"Our world of digital devices and the accompanying devastation to meaningful personal relationships has been over-documented by now. But we need grounded, practical ways to cultivate and maintain the most important relationships in our lives while taking the reality of our screen-driven lives into account. Dr. Bennett guides us into the principles, practices, and questions that enable us to build (or rebuild) close personal relationships characterized by presence, trust, and love. She leads us into the unchangeable, difficult world of attentiveness with grace upon which flawed, sinful human beings can participate in reconciled, redemptive relationships within the deep horizons of enduring love."

—**Calvin L. Troup**, President, Geneva College, Pennsylvania

"This is no ordinary textbook or relationship development book. Written in Dr. Bennett's poetic, almost philosophical style, the reader is encouraged to consider multiple aspects of current relational challenges. Contrasting enduring, faith-filled relationships with popular media depictions motivates the reader to reflect on their own notions of love, communication, sexuality, and the influence of digital culture. Each thoughtful chapter concludes with questions making this book appropriate for college courses, support groups, and individual reading. The ideas touch on valuable insights for any stage of relational development but align them with biblical principles. As someone who married young and has been with my partner for over 50 years filled with the good, the bad, and the ugly of long-term relationships, I still found pearls of wisdom in this thoughtful exploration of relationships. Thank you, Stephanie."

—**Karen Lollar**, PhD, Professor Emeritus, Metropolitan State University of Denver

"Our rapidly changing media environment demands that we consciously learn to communicate meaningfully with each other, especially in love. *Relationships on the Run* provides a guide by developing simple injunctions like "pay attention," "be there," "be realistic," "listen," "converse," "be affectionate," "know yourself," "surrender," "find grace in conflict," "repair what's broken," "know silence," and "pray always." Solid Christian teaching, research evidence, and examples flesh each of these out, making this book both a wonderful resource and a trustworthy guide."

—**Paul A. Soukup**, SJ, Professor of Communication, Santa Clara University

"Reading this delightful encouragement to build healthy relationships refreshes the soul. One imagines sitting with the author over coffee, seeking and receiving wise counsel. Dr. Bennett's clear, direct writing addresses issues of today that haunt most of us. Rooted in a relationship with Jesus Christ, she guides us through challenges, technological distractions, and conflict. Her grace and joy shine through as we track key tools like humility, presence, and confession. This book is a gem that you'll want to return to often."

—**Annalee R. Ward**, PhD, Director Emerita, Wendt Character Initiative, University of Dubuque

"In a world filled with constant demands for our attention and superficial displays of love, Bennett highlights the beauty of living intentionally with our Creator and those around us. Her wisdom is deeply rooted in biblical truth and a passion for pursuing fulfilling relationships."

—**Kevyn Freehill**, Market Segment Coordinator, Roebbelen Contracting, Inc.

"Dr. Stephanie Bennett authors a timely book filled with powerful words of wisdom. This work speaks directly to our technological culture. She presents clear and persuasive arguments, advocating for personal and social engagement in communication inspired by the virtue of love. Dr. Bennett's insights are grounded in principles of spiritual formation and a well-established faith tradition. She stresses that without sincere love there can be no authentic communication. I highly recommend this work for anyone who seeks deeper relational communication and meaningful personal interaction and engagement with others."

—**Terriel R. Byrd**, PhD, Lead Pastor, Living Word Christian Community, and Professor Emeritus, Palm Beach Atlantic University

"In a technological society characterized by social media and iPhone culture, nothing is more critical than helping people develop authentic, loving relationships. Our students and society at large are grappling with anxiety, loneliness, depression, and incivility. In her book on fostering relationships, my good friend and colleague, Dr. Stephanie Bennett, offers a beautifully written, insightful, and essential resource for such a time as this."

—**Geraldine E. Forsberg**, PhD, Senior Instructor, Western Washington University; Co-President of the International Jacques Ellul Society

"In this book, Dr. Bennett addresses a complex issue: the impact of chronic partial attention on our love relationships. She successfully translates this issue into the common language of our time. She exposes the emotional vampires that we have become, satisfied with the counterfeit quality time in the guise of social media. Dr. Bennett clarifies that one does not get quality time in a relationship without the component of in-person quantity time. Even my young grandchildren know that love is spelled T-I-M-E with Mimi."

—**Jackie Kendall**, author of *Lady in Waiting*

"Dr. Stephanie Bennett offers a refreshing call to authenticity in a world filled with distractions. Her writing inspires us to pause, reflect, and seek a higher, more meaningful way of living. With keen insight, she encourages a mindset that fosters genuine connection, authentic love, and richer relationships—an essential message in our increasingly digital age."

—**Joseph Sowers**, PhD, Assistant Professor of Communication, Palm Beach Atlantic University

"My colleague Stephanie Bennett offers us much distilled wisdom and many rich insights for communication and relationships in our distracted, anxious, increasingly detached social media culture. This book is readable, realistic, honest, and practical. It also challenges false ideas about identity and relationships and inspires readers to do the hard work of shifting priorities, reordering their worlds, and redoubling their efforts to deepen their connections with God and with others."

—**Paul Copan**, PhD, Pledger Family Chair of Philosophy and Ethics, Palm Beach Atlantic University

"Bennett's *Relationships on the Run* promises a lot—and delivers! Her analysis of today's culture of social media, distraction, and the replacement of healthy, positive, embodied human relationships with superficial interactions is spot-on. Her extended, detailed prescriptions for the discovery or recovery of deep, enduring, positive communication and life together are a rich treasure trove of insights from the author's lifetime of study and experience. This is nothing less than a great feast for readers of all ages and life situations."

—**David W. Gill**, PhD, Retired Professor of Christian Ethics, Gordon-Conwell Theological Seminary

"Using words and stories almost magically, Stephanie Bennett invites us into a world where hope abounds for friendships, marriages, and families facing relational difficulties. Although communication skills are crucial, hope rests on God's love for us and our willingness to seek the Lord to discern how best to move forward. *Relationships on the Run* addresses the complex relational challenges of our fast-paced, digital-driven world and provides biblically grounded, practical ways to rise above them. A must-read for all, including my students! I am eager for them to learn from the wisdom shared in this book."

—**Diane M. Badzinski**, PhD, Professor of Communication, Colorado Christian University

Relationships On the Run

How to Grow Authentic Connections
and Lasting Intimacy in a Hurried Culture

Relationships On the Run

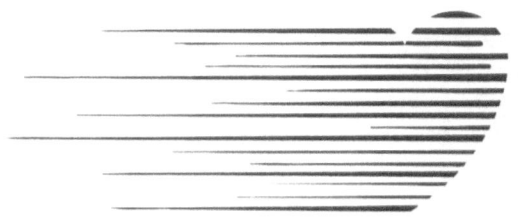

How to Grow Authentic Connections and Lasting Intimacy in a Hurried Culture

STEPHANIE BENNETT

Integratio Press
Pasco, Washington

This is a publication of Foundations, a Division of Integratio Press.

integratiopress.com

Integratio Press is an Imprint of the Christianity and Communication Studies Network.
11503 Easton Dr.
Pasco, WA 99301

www.theccsn.com

Cover design: Carol O'Callaghan
Interior design: Carol O'Callaghan

paperback isbn: 978-1-959685-37-1
ebook isbn: 978-1-959685-38-8

Library of Congress Control Number available from the publisher.

*This book is dedicated to the many people who
have encouraged me along the way. Starting with
mentors in my graduate studies, including Eleanor Novak,
Cliff Christians, Jack Keeler, and many other professors who
contributed to my life. Especially my one and only mother,
Marylou Margaret Renzo Fitzpatrick,
who knew long before it came to pass, that
I would find purpose and joy in the classroom.*

Table of Contents

Acknowledgements

THIS BOOK would not have been possible without the many people who took an interest and encouraged me along the way. Beginning with mentors in my graduate studies, like Eleanor Novak, who somehow knew I would go on to a PhD long before I did; Jack Keeler, whose spiritual grounding and tireless input helped shape my early research; Cliff Christians, who has been like a father to me; Quentin Schultze, Michael Graves, Darlene Graves, and so many other professors who modeled an active life of scholarship right alongside true love and care for their students. Thanks, as well, to all the fine friends and scholars who contributed their slice of life in each chapter's breakout boxes. What a gift!

Special thanks to executive editor, Diane Badizinski, whose positivity and support was vital, especially in this book's early drafts. Thanks also to Denise Edwards Neff for her feedback on early drafts of the book, and to Jessica McFarland and all the folks at Integratio Press who helped this project make its way to completion.

And then there is Mr. Bennett, the one I have spent forty years with: talking, listening, loving, and living life through each season of life. His respect for my work and support have been undying. Thank you, Earl.

Foreword

RELATIONSHIPS make us rich.

And of course, by that I mean the good ones. Relationships that set us at ease, allow us to explore our own journey alongside others, and reward authenticity and vulnerability are the true riches of our humanity. To share the struggles and challenges of living in the twenty-first century with mutual compassion and encouragement and to celebrate joy, however we find it, with good friends, gives life deep meaning and fulfillment.

My greatest joys have all been inside close, meaningful relationships. But to be honest, they have also been the source of my deepest anguish. When relationships are good, they are incredibly good, but when they turn manipulative or destructive, especially with people you care about, they cause untold pain. And yet, I have found that the joy of the former easily outweighs the risk of the latter.

The trick is learning to manage our relationships wisely, cultivating those that nourish our spirit, limiting our expectations so we make room for human weakness, repairing those we can that have been damaged and, when necessary, creating boundaries for those fraught with insecurity, jealousy, dishonesty, or threatening behaviors.

Relationships used to be far less complicated in the last century when I grew up. We weren't hounded by social media or encouraged to brand ourselves. Most people we met lived down the street from us or were visible in our community. Character was more important than image. We held a lot of beliefs and passions in common and it was far easier to connect.

But the lines for healthy relationships have shifted in recent decades. Living authentically and vulnerably has never been more terrifying and the things that can suddenly take a relationship sideways are often unforeseen. Our society rewards achievement over friendships and amusement over community; consequently, healthy relationships aren't always easy to find.

You hold in your hands a masterful work that will help you find and cultivate the kind of relationships that will make your life rich and rewarding. I couldn't recommend this book highly enough. There are few opportunities to help us discover how healthy relationships work and to avoid the pitfalls that cause harm. You now hold one of those in your hands.

Your guide on this journey is Stephanie Bennett, a researcher and college professor specializing in communication and media ecology. She has a deep understanding of the power of healthy relationships. This isn't just her academic pursuit; this is her life. Stephanie has been my friend for nearly thirty years. And even though we live on opposite coasts, we have found occasion to cross paths somewhere in the world and explore our combined passion for a relationship with God that's transforming and connections with people that offer a continual resource of wisdom and encouragement. She can help you appreciate the power of relationships and find ways to explore them joyfully.

What I respect most about Stephanie is that her words and her life synch up as a beautiful and authentic symphony. That's not true of every writer I know; many espouse things for others they don't aspire to themselves. I have seen her commitment to loving relationships inside her own family as a wife and mother, but also well beyond it to a wide circle of friendships. And this isn't just in good times; I've seen her deal with difficult relationships, and she always finds a way to enhance the lives of others around her. I've watched her navigate crisis and heartache and have been a benefactor of her love and graciousness in my own times of struggle.

That's what I appreciate most about writers I enjoy. I don't look for perfection; we all have our blind spots and weaknesses. People don't have to be successful, humorous, or well-connected. I want them to be real—to enjoy what they enjoy, have the vulnerability to struggle where they struggle, and the curiosity to question what they need to question while respecting that same process in others.

For me, genuineness is even more important when someone puts thoughts to paper for others to consider. Words are empty if they aren't backed by a life that reflects them. Rest assured that these words are backed up by a kind and conscientious heart.

So more than recommending her thoughts to you, let me commend the woman herself. She's as genuine a person as I'm pleased to know. Her compass is locked on a purpose greater than herself and that informs her actions and her graciousness to others.

As she shares the things that she has learned, you can rest assured she speaks from a reservoir of wisdom she has gained through personal experience. Her wisdom is enlightening, her passion for Jesus contagious, her ethics exemplary, and her faith deep and abiding.

This is the wisdom of a woman who means them. I trust they will enrich and inspire you as much as her life has touched mine.

Wayne Jacobsen
Author of *He Loves Me* and *So You Don't Want to Go to Church Anymore*, and co-author of *The Shack*

Preface

STEPHANIE BENNETT'S NEW BOOK tackles a subject that we all need to consider—how to form real relationships in a world of chaotic, superficial, on-the-run messaging. Moreover, her book is a heartfelt look at how we all can flourish without giving up on new technologies and hiding from interpersonal challenges.

Bennett understands Jesus's observation that our words ultimately come from our hearts. All of our communication reveals our hearts in motion. So does our lack of communication, when our hearts shut down and our relationships wither away. Our motion turns inward, away from others. We even become resentful toward those who do not seem to like or love us.

Do you want to enjoy deep friends and loved ones? Then get your heart into the game of life. Open up. Risk looking like a fool or, worse yet, being rejected. As Bennett explains, there is no short cut to heartfelt communion with others. Relationships are a daily matter of whole-hearted investment in interpersonal communication.

In this book, Bennett wears her own heart on her words. The result is an inspirational series of stories from her own life that act like parables of communicative hope for all of us. It is the kind of book that you do not want to put down because her heart connects with your heart. She sheds warm light on the darker shadows and deeper concerns of our hearts. You can feel her compassion in every chapter.

All around us, communication is falling apart. I call it "communicative entropy." Consequently, our relationships are dissolving as well. We live amidst shallow word salads and destructive word bombs that carry little relational hope. We feel alienated and even hurt. All of us. We just do not like to admit it. We hope for real love, for instance, but we barely know how to form devoted relationships. This might be the greatest social irony of our time: abundant messaging but very little life-giving communion with one another, God, and ourselves.

To meet Stephanie Bennett in person is to discover that she has somehow managed to keep her heart in her listening and speaking. She is there—present. She is emotive, empathetic, and encouraging. You can feel her enthusiasm and joy in tender interactions. You can also feel her pain when she openly discusses some of the deepest trials she has faced in her own life. Fortunately for us, she describes her challenges in this book. She ties her talk about communication to her life experiences. The book becomes a series of parables that show us all how to live with heart even when we are discouraged and overly busy.

So if you want to taste real relationships, this is your book. If you want to experience authentic friendships and romances, this is your book. Let the author take you on a journey into real communion with God, others, and yourself. You will be blessed, just as I have been by knowing the author and reading her book of heartfelt wisdom about forming authentic relationship on the run.

Quentin J. Schultze, PhD
Professor Emeritus of Communication, Calvin University

Introduction

WHEN IT COMES to human relationships, it has been said that communication is everything. While I'd be the first to say communication is key to a lively, lovely, lasting relationship, the "everything" part is a bit overstated. Each person brings to the other a unique and largely hidden self that becomes part of the fertile ground upon which a relationship might grow or one that remains hidden, masked, and bound for confusing cyclical demise. Whether it's two friends forming a deeper trust between them, adolescent siblings sharing the same room, a married couple navigating the new waters of parenthood, or even business partners learning each other's strengths and weaknesses, strong communication skills will add much to a relationship's resiliency, but to walk in the wisdom and enjoyment of relationships that flourish—and last—there is so much more to consider.

The first to consider is the place of love in our relationships. Love isn't just a value-add to a life of work. Life is all about love. It's life's most important feature. My goal in writing is to help readers move from relationships that may be built on a faulty foundation and fraught with difficulty to those that flourish and flower as a result of learning to keep the love of God central in all things. Today, 15 years after writing my first book about cultivating long-lasting, loving relationships, we find ourselves in one of those points in history when great shifts in culture are taking place. The way we conduct our primary relationships is quite different from previous eras.

The ubiquitous constant presence of our personal mobile media (PMM) (i.e., all the devices and programs that allow us to communicate "on the run") reveal new relational pitfalls. Impediments associated with social media, artificial intelligence, and so many other emerging technologies surround us, often circumventing our best efforts to make our relationships a priority. The pervasive, all-encompassing reach of the Internet has left many relationships in ruin as so many are unprepared for its addictive properties.

While most people now know not to accept an email from a Nigerian prince asking for money or believe a flattering request from the ideal mate who is really on a stealthy catfishing expedition, there are still many hazards to address. Ethical problems abound in every sector of society. College coursework can be conducted via smartphone with very little interaction between class members, making it possible to garner a degree remotely, but losing the sense of community and collective gain you can find in a traditional classroom. Potential mates are to be found on the Internet, but the addictive properties of social media and the ensuing lack of presence can make it difficult to stay faithful.

Everything has changed, but nothing has changed. Students still feel the demand of a paper deadline; young lovers are still getting married, the globe keeps on turning, and we're all still longing to make meaning out of our lives. Using digital devices without considering what's most appropriate for the situation leads to frustration that too easily leads to communication breakdown, and that can often sadly lead to the end of a relationship. It's here that the real problems with our media-saturated society are largely hidden, and it's here that they begin to emerge. Throughout this book we ask questions familiar to so many of us. Is there hope for a friendship when a confidence is broken, especially if personal information or images are spread throughout social media? Can a couple recover from a breach in fidelity? What if that breach is limited to emotional involvement in on-line spaces or via text messaging? How about relationships in the work-place? Can you ever trust your co-worker again if he or she forwarded your private email to your boss or the entire department? What can you do to demonstrate kindness, thoughtfulness, and care to a colleague when self-centeredness is the only thing returned? These are among the many relational quagmires addressed in this book, those potholes on old roads that are so often cloaked from our view until we fall into them.

Relationships on the Run is a book that attempts to provide encour-agement as well as a map to navigate the choppy waters of change in communication practices, offering ways to find and maintain close social relationships. Many of these practices involve time-tested, overlapping skills such as listening carefully, keeping a heart-attitude that's open, and learning to use nonverbal communication cues appropriately and well. You'll find these and other basic communication skills woven throughout all the pages, with the individual chapters focusing on greater detail and depth.

My primary aim is to point to a path that leads to rich relationships, grounded in grace and the love of God; to help readers see, feel, and truly *know* the joy of walking in healthy relationships that flourish and grow in-stead of flounder and fail. The road signs to this life aren't always clear or even present, but the communicational tools necessary to follow along this path are readily available. Much of what's needed to remain on this path has been altered significantly by a media environment that's dominated by digital devices and other technological tools that automate and abbreviate our words and their meanings. These changes will factor in our discussion of relational fruitfulness, but technology isn't the foundation of what I am offering here. The gift of God's love to us and the ability to love others is what everything else rests on. And while this key opens the door to rich, satisfying relationships, no formula for success exists. No definitive list is to be found. Every relationship is different, and what's most needed is a heart that's willing to seek the Lord for discernment.

But there are communication skills that play a crucial role in establishing such richness, and here I've attempted to share the most significant ones. The first three chapters emphasize some of the challenges to relationships that are amplified in this age of massive inter-connectivity and digital reliance. We'll discuss the ways our personal mobile media (PMM) reconfigure our days, reshape our knowledge of ourselves, and create an entirely new environment in which we communicate. Our smartphones, tablets, and wearable digital devices are no longer novel; they are ubiquitous and ever emerging with updates, new uses, better cameras and video, cool programs, and seemingly endless possibilities. We'll explore ways to use them that lead to life-giving relationships and where to use the most restraint. Then, in chapters 3 through 10, we'll drill down into the tried-and-true skills needed to communicate well and uncover several issues that thwart them.

These skills involve many overlapping elements of excellent communication such as listening, openness and vulnerability, identity, intimacy, affection, resolving conflict, and the art of conversation. While the work of God in our relationships is threaded throughout the whole book, the last two chapters zero in on the importance of bringing our faith into our relationships. First is the need to recognize the power of the nonverbal realm of communication, including the way that silence "speaks" in moments of devotion, tears, tumult, and listening. Finally, the place of prayer; specifically, the way it can shape our relationships. While the love of God implicitly grounds the entire book, Chapter 12 considers more specifically the way prayer impacts the degree to which our relationships flourish. No matter how strenuous or challenging, the Spirit of God can move mountains to renew and restore relationships that have become stale or lifeless. I've seen it in my own relationships and among those who have come to me for relationship coaching.

If you've ever been tempted to give up on the idea of love, take a deep breath, pour yourself a cup of coffee or tea, and find a few minutes of quiet to begin reading. I invite you to join the conversation, one that's been going on probably since the beginning of time. Ask the Holy Spirit to traverse with you through this book as I share some of the lessons He has taught me—lessons I'm still learning. I pray you will read the pages that follow as a topic that's not only important to us all, but perhaps the very core of what it means to be human. Relationships are so natural and basic that they can be easily overlooked. This is the simplicity, beauty, and fundamental power of love as it blossoms and matures in all varieties of relationships.

Chapter 1

Understanding the Pitfalls of
Mediated Multitasking

Outdo one another in honoring each other.
— Romans 12:10b, ESV

IT WAS 1997. The flip phone in my pocket vibrated, alerting me that my husband's plane landed in Minneapolis. I didn't have to wait to get home to check my message machine. I could finish my workout with the peaceful knowledge that he had arrived safely.

Back then, most of us were just getting accustomed to staying in digital touch with loved ones. The novel freedom of mobile phones and texting while engaged in activities like watching ball games or going for a walk was wonderful. We could quickly text a friend in another state just to say hello without sending a letter, making an intrusive call, or composing an email. It was all new and exciting. We didn't realize that the quickened pace of the twentieth century was just about to take a giant leap, radically altering our lives. This new pace was changing our life's rhythms, especially our relationships. We were entering a new world of high-speed, non-stop messaging.

Fast-forward to today. Smart phones dominate our relationships. Much of our interaction with loved ones occurs on the run, in bits and pieces, not face-to-face. We're so accustomed to multitasking that we forget to focus on relationships. Amit Sood, author of *The Mayo Clinic Guide to Stress-free Living*, says that such multitasking can hurt our relationships: "It's not about the amount of time that you give other people," he notes, "it's the amount of 'you' in that time."[1]

In this chapter, I look more closely at the trade-offs between rapid-fire messaging and slower, but more fulfilling, communion with one another. There are many factors, but the increased pace of living set by these new tools of communication is essential. When we rush through our days, it's nearly impossible to be fully present to each other. We must do all we can to avoid the dangerous development of a multitasking mindset. Another factor is social saturation, which happens when our social circle becomes cluttered with more names and dates than we can reasonably manage. Each of these developments causes much disarray in our lives, especially relational dysfunction.

Pace

Maintaining our relationships on the run initially seems easy and practical, but we pay a price for the convenience. We feel scattered, stressed, and even lonely while our messages fly into and out of our devices. The promise of fulfilling friendships and marriages is illusory. We struggle to sustain meaningful, intimate relationships with the people we most want to love. The rhythm of non-stop messaging replaces the rhythm of relational joy and delight.

We need to consider an essential life truth: "Technology giveth and technology taketh away."[2] Technological gifts, like smart phones, don't merely add a little something new and beneficial to our lives. They change nearly everything, including how we think and act.[3] Our digital devices affect our sleep, recreation, and especially our relationships. We feel like we need to be messaging all the time. We lose the more traditional ways to meet people and maintain closeness.

Our smartphones, wearables, tablets, and other PMM have supercharged our lives. The daily rhythm of life is dizzying, weakening love and long-term relationships.[4] Long before the debilitating effects of the COVID-19 pandemic, studies showed an increase in mental health disorders and an exponential rise in loneliness.[5] The connection between our digital devices and these issues is complex, but one element is the heightened pace of life and the often overwhelming pressure to simply keep up.

After the height of the COVID-19 pandemic, psychologists and physicians continued to see even more young people with anxiety disorders. This decline in public health—coupled with the political divide and growing lack of civility in the U.S.—contributed to relational problems. While many mental health issues are rooted in financial and emotional stress, a primary factor is feelings of isolation. A study of the exponential rise in anxiety disorders after COVID-19 found that 69% of students who considered stopping their coursework cited emotional stress as a reason.[6] The finding corresponds with many similar studies, with children and young adults representing the bulk of the growth in these disorders.[7]

Even before COVID-19, studies pointed to the constant and pervasive use of our PMM as a factor in increased depression and isolation among those who depend upon social media and texting for their interpersonal communication.[8] Now, decades after my flip phone alerted me to my spouse's safe arrival in the Twin Cities, smartphones affect all of our indispensable relationships by speeding up our messaging without deepening our interactions. Whether it's in friendship, family, or marriage relationships, maintaining closeness is now more challenging. We feel lonely and scattered without the rhythms of regular, consistent physical presence. The rhythm of messaging replaces the more intimate rhythm of in-person conversation.

We live in a media environment that's populated by social networks and algorithms that radically readjust our relational context, upending the rhythm that we need to flourish relationally. Although our personal mobile media are helpful in many ways, overdependence on them crowds out essential practices such as paying attention to one another, listening, eye contact, and touching. Digital devices allow us to connect with each other at great distances, but they can separate us from more personal contact with those we love.

Meaningful dialogue is difficult in our hurried lives. Texting may help us exchange quick bits of information, but the brevity and missing nonverbal communication cues make these tools insufficient to develop, grow, and maintain our primary relationships. Receiving a text message from my husband upon his airport arrival isn't the same as greeting him, hugging him, sitting down together for coffee, and looking into each other's eyes as we converse about recent experiences.

Today, sending messages replaces deeper demonstrations of love. It's easy to fall into the habit of not expressing the affection we feel for others. Our relationships drift apart.

Countless divorces and broken relationships are the result of such relational neglect. I'm still amazed when I hear a person claim his divorce came out of the blue, or that he just didn't know his spouse anymore, even though they've been texting daily. No matter how strongly we feel love for a person, that love must be expressed regularly, especially in person, without distractions. Our best intentions can't make up for communicating such affection with time and presence. In other words, the pace of digital life can push us away from our best intentions.

Perhaps it's the morning kiss at the front door as your spouse heads to work, but you check to see who is texting you, or if there's a text from a colleague. Maybe the gentle squeeze of a friend's hand would've done wonders to bolster her confidence at the new job, but "look at the time!" Could it be that we need to stop looking so intensely at our screens and more closely into the eyes of those we love? Even if it's in the cracks and crevices of the day, communicating affection requires untethered time and space: "It is imperative to physical and mental health that humans give and receive affectionate expressions."[9] The speed and mobility of our devices certainly can help us get together for affection, but we must do so intentionally and in the rhythm of relationship. Love grows when it's expressed. Without attending to the rhythms of affection we can easily drift apart into loneliness, no matter how many messages we're sending and receiving. Love that flourishes takes time and focus.

Multitasking Our Way to Chaos

"Please give me your partial attention." Can you imagine saying such a thing to your spouse or friend? Do any of us expect anything less than full attention from those with whom we're in a close relationship? Deep and satisfying relationships require adequate time, energy, and focus. Otherwise, they tend to fizzle out. Our multitasking mentality contributes to this dysfunction. The most rewarding relationships require single-tasking.

Some of us seem naturally better at multitasking than others, but the value of multitasking is grossly overrated. The ability to throw clothes in a washer with a baby on your hip or while chatting with a friend on the phone is great, but that's different from comparing prices on three websites while driving a car, giving directions to a friend about your estimated time of arrival, texting a last-minute message, and choosing a new playlist for the trip. The latter is interaction with media, not a person. It also creates a habit of continuous partial attention (CPA). CPA is a way of being busy, interacting with your media environment rather than relating.[10] Over time, this excessive multitasking with personal mobile devices is both physically and relationally dangerous. It leads to auto accidents and relational decline. My point is that we can't cultivate loving relationships by multitasking our way through life. The most rewarding relationships require time and attention, usually one person at a time. Otherwise, our relationships tend to crash and burn.

The temptation to multitask our way through life is caused partly by the expanded mediated landscape.[11] We should enjoy using our social media, email, and websites; they offer opportunities for connection with others. But managing them all can overwhelm us. Instead of having a few close friends and siblings whose birthdays we like to remember and celebrate, we have dozens or even hundreds of persons we barely know. It can create a pressure that adds to the information flood already at our doorstep. Such social saturation presents a potential crisis in intimacy and commitment.[12]

Slowing to Her Pace

My wife, Sara, had some undiagnosed trauma that surfaced late in her life. Without warning, she left me while I was on a business trip on the advice of a therapist who assumed she must have been married to an abusive husband. I had no idea why she had left me and she wouldn't communicate with me for four weeks. During that time, I would often go into the beautiful English garden she had created in our backyard. I felt closer to her there than anywhere else, and there, I could pray and consider what God might do to bring us back together.

As I tended to her earthly garden, I prayed God would tend to her heart. One day, in my haste to pull a weed just out of reach, I lost my balance. When I threw my foot out to keep from falling, it broke a stalk of irises in full bloom. As I looked at the destroyed flowers, there was no way to put them back together. My heart hurt as if I'd broken something in Sara. At that moment God's Spirit spoke to my heart: "You need to slow down." It wasn't just about pulling weeds, it was also about how I drive, rush about the kitchen when we're preparing supper, and make decisions quicker than my wife can contemplate them.

When Sara finally came back, I had three weeks of practice slowing my pace to meet hers. It proved to be a major factor in God healing the brokenness in Sara's heart and our relationship. You can't walk with someone if you're always ahead of them trying to hurry them along. Walk at someone else's pace if you want the relationship to grow and soon you will find a rhythm together that will work well for both of you.

— Wayne Jacobsen, Author of *He Loves Me* and *So You Don't Want to Go to Church Anymore*, and co-author of *The Shack*

Social Saturation

Social saturation is a result of the Information Age. It's like a sponge that needs to be squeezed. It's already taken in too much water and if you keep using it, it makes more of a mess than when you began. The sponge works well when used as it should but has limited functionality. Our lives similarly become full, overwhelmed. Our primary relationships fall apart because we're trying to manage too many commitments, names, and dates; too much of everything presses in on us. Anthropologist Robin Dunbar says that the average person can only satisfactorily manage 150 relationships.[13] But "managing" isn't the same as focusing on a few key relationships.

The larger our social network, the weaker our most personal connections. We drown in the countless new points of connection, the ever expanding network of social ties, and seemingly endless list of passwords and apps. This firehose of information pouring into each of us produces excessive stimuli, mental confusion, emotional stress, and unmanageable schedules. The results are stress and anxiety.[14] We might believe that we're just "too busy," but our bodies know. Our hearts know. Our digestive tracks know. Our respiratory systems know. The over-stimulation of our nervous system can wreak havoc on our physical systems, and our relationships often pay the price.[15]

Stress of this sort impacts our most significant, primary relationships. Our many connections may be quite enjoyable, the information may be interesting, and some of the messages may help us understand the world around us. Still, time spent scrolling through these wide and mostly shallow "interactions" reduces the time we can invest in the most important people in our lives.

Meanwhile, our global media fills our days and weeks with posting, scrolling, and reacting to bite-sized messages. Time spent managing our social networking certainly affords new opportunities for connection with others, but as we embrace them our lives are apt to become overwhelmed with managing them. Now, instead of having several close friends and siblings whose birthdays we like to remember, our reach has expanded to many times that amount. We wonder why lifelong friendships have simply faded away. We're puzzled why a close friend, fiancé, or spouse have become distant. We regret our shrinking sense of community.

Reclaiming Meandering Moments

Social psychologist Kenneth Gergen suggests what's needed to address this problem is to get back in touch with moments of leisure where we're not rushing, not multitasking, but taking time to pay attention to our lives. In these moments, we put our drive to be productive on hold and become more intentional to keep our daily pace in check. We need these unscheduled, "meandering" moments "to develop 'best friends' . . . who can be fully trusted or relied upon during a time of need."[16]

It's hard to nurture a real relationship when we're in constant social networking motion. We're just firing messages back and forth when, instead, we need to spend time with others, converse with them, laugh together, and learn how to meander into the joy of playful interactions. "Under these conditions," as Gergen observes, "even the very concept of 'closest' or 'best' friend undergoes a sea change. Rather than living in a communion of souls, we're always playing 'catch-up.' We lose the capacity for genuine friendship."[17]

Such meandering moments disappear in a world of digital multitasking. Relationships need these in-person moments. I like to think of these as the "cracks and crevices" of the day—the moments that come between everything else, such as mealtimes, coffee breaks, walking together to and from work or classes, and chatting together after worship. We can also use these moments to converse, to offer a prayer for our loved ones, or to send a quick text to someone we're thinking about. Or we can do what so many of us do: scroll. Time spent scrolling has risen exponentially. Many young people say they scroll through social media and are on their phones constantly. They admit spending too much time doing so.[18] Some studies point to the physical and psychological dangers of excessive scrolling.[19] Making time to say hello with a phone call or a text helps keep friends and spouses connected. A short message is a reminder of that connection, and an important countermeasure to the problem of social saturation and overuse of digital media.

Another example relates to public civility and engagement with our neighbors. People we meet on public transportation, a receptionist at the doctor's office, a cashier at the supermarket; these aren't primary relationships, but they are part of our social network. Our ties with them are weak, but the small, seemingly insignificant social interactions are important.[20] Acknowledging another person in a public setting through eye contact, small talk, and nonverbal expression is a regular reminder of our common humanness. Something as natural as a smile and hello are small but significant ways to affirm our shared humanness. Actually, "even weak ties allow distant clusters of people to access novel information that can lead to new opportunities, innovation, and increased productivity."[21] Interactions with members of our community help us feel a part of a place and stay connected.

Some technologies help address our longing to be connected with those we love, especially when separated by long distances or extended time apart. I am grateful to use these tools to chat with lifelong friends who live far away. What a blessing to engage with loved ones in screen-mediated communication. Still, the screen does not satisfy my need for unplanned meandering and especially for hugs.[22]

Restoring healthy rhythms of a relationship requires a real change in mindset, especially acknowledging our addiction to multitasking. We need a mindset that views every person as made in the image of God, created by a loving maker. Thus, each person is worthy of eye contact, or a smile, a good word. It's an attitude that recognizes the worth of others and finds respect in the commonality of our humanness. Living in this mindset provides an essential start in helping our primary relationships thrive. Living in such a renewed flow of love and grace is the undercurrent necessary to maintain strong and healthy relationships.

To create this positive flow requires more than just desire. It will take creating new habits that foster relationships in the "in between" moments of each day. I can imagine what our beloved Apostle Paul must have felt when he said, "Further, my brothers and sisters rejoice in the Lord! It is no trouble for me to write the same things to you again, and it is safeguard for you," for I must reiterate the importance of fostering the flow of relationship (Phil. 3:1, NIV). Attentiveness to the small snatches of time can help us stay awake—fully present—to ourselves and our loved ones, even more so than the occasional weekend away or special event.

Conclusion

Because we're made for relationships, most of us continue to long for those relationships that bless and satisfy the deepest social, emotional, and physical needs at the core of our souls. We want friendships, marriages, and families that add fullness to life that makes all our trials worthwhile. These longings are attainable, but we must remember several important realities about the tools we're using to communicate and be sure to stay aware of them. The next chapter brings our discussion to the most basic ingredient for cultivating close relationships—the importance of simply being present.

Questions for Reflection

1. Consider the depth of your friendships, family, and romantic relationships. To what extent do the three factors (pace, multitasking, social saturation) affect your relationships? What factor affects your relationships the most?

2. What two or three measures might you take to guard against the corrosion of your most important relationships?

3. Consider how the addictive properties of some social media, digital games, or platforms such as Zoom, Teams, and FaceTime might help or hinder your relationship with God and his people. Apply this to your own life and take a few minutes to write this in your personal journal.

Chapter 2

Feeling the Power of Presence

You make known to me the path of life; in your presence there is fullness of joy, at your right hand are pleasures forevermore.
— Psalm 16:11, ESV

WHEN I FIRST heard someone say "the ears are the sexiest part of the human body," I was at an academic conference in Chicago, sitting across from a notable communication scholar whose life was dedicated to studying the mystery of the spoken word. What did he mean? Our conversation proved to be one of the most significant of my academic years.

As if in suspended animation, his words hovered like a drone in the air between us. He was in his early eighties; I was in my late thirties. We were sharing a cup of coffee and our thoughts about how romantic relationships evolve. When I finally got the courage to ask him what he meant about the ears, his answer was quite simple: "A man speaks from the depth of his interior into the depth of a woman's. Words of love are spoken, and intimacy begins."

Still, I was curious about how he remained interested in a subject like the spoken word. My own preferred mode of communication had long been writing, mostly because of the ability to be more reflective when writing. Besides, speaking creates much more opportunity to get flustered, and who likes that? Spoken words scared me a bit; written words gave me confidence. Sexy ears and spoken words? Where was the conversation headed?

He patiently answered my questions. He shared stories of the many interviews and experiments he conducted involving the acquisition of speech and the significance of spoken words in relationships. In fact, his own words touched my heart and opened my mind. The way he spoke to my ears convinced me that I needed to study and share the importance of the human voice to nurture relationships. One of the most eye-opening aspects of his work was in the physiology of the spoken word. He found that the voice is integral in every way to the health of all our relationships.

Realizing the significance of the human voice as a powerful agent in meaning-making, in negotiating, and intimacy—well, it soon became one of my favorite subjects.

I still greatly appreciate the power of the written word. I now realize that writing can overly intellectualize words, taking the breath and presence right out of it. By contrast, the voice is like a magic carpet. Through voice, our words flow forth on the wings of our breath, emanating from deep within our hearts, flying into others' souls. Whether consciously or subconsciously, the spoken word can penetrate the outer skin and settle into our hearts for a lifetime. I'll never forget that phrase, sexy ears.

In this chapter I look at the power of presence, and the connection between voice and affection. I also examine the ways technologies have shaped us, and the need to adapt to change without losing the power of speech.

Speaking of Love

Spoken words have the power to enhance our relationships through physical and emotional intimacy. This knitting together of verbal and nonverbal communication creates a sturdier ground—a stronger foundation for love to flourish. Professor Kory Floyd, who studies affection between the sexes in friendship and parent-child relationships, says that the amount of verbal, direct nonverbal, and support-based affectionate communication characterizing the relationships is "directly associated" with relational closeness, liking and love, relationship satisfaction and communication satisfaction.[1] In other words, what we say can bring us together as well as tear us apart. Words can cause a harsh rift in a relationship, but they can also draw the other out.

The importance of the spoken word and physical presence may be the most significant in a marriage relationship. Although sexual union between a husband and wife is a gift that can bring the couple into deeper intimacy, without the willingness to communicate from one heart to another, emotional closeness is limited. It doesn't matter how frequently the two engage in physical union; without sharing heart-to-heart, the truest, most complete sense of intimacy will remain unfulfilled. To move toward greater emotional intimacy and bonding, couples must push past the tendency to self-protect and overcome their fear of emotional openness. Communicating love verbally and nonverbally is essential.

Perhaps the most basic element in romantic relationships is simply the desire to be with the other. To be present. It's not terribly complicated. Couples who long to know each other more fully must be willing to spend the time together, and this isn't burdensome. Most find a way to do it. This doesn't require spending thousands of dollars on counseling or expensive adventures on land or on sea. We do, however, need to be in each other's physical presence. We need to hear and fully listen to each other. This is necessary because "of its very nature, the sound world has a depth, dimension, and fullness such as the visual, despite its own distinctive beauties, can never achieve."[2] Can intimate relationships flourish between those who are deaf and can't hear the sound of the other's voice? By all means, yes. Here we're not discussing exceptions, however, but exploring the practices adults with fully operational auditory functions experience.

Voice. Breath. Life.

Despite the power of being present with one another, we may still find ourselves failing if we take the power of the voice for granted. The voice flows from the breath of our mouth. Voice indicates life. Our current ability to detach voice from physical presence notwithstanding, hearing someone's voice in person is far different than hearing on the mobile phone or via video. There is the matter of breath and the matter of the heart. Calling from deep within one person to the depth of the other, words more easily slip out, without a filter, revealing what's in our hearts. This makes words a powerful medium for healing, comfort, and nurture.

But the power of the spoken word works just as intensely in harmful ways. When words of bitterness and hate are spoken, they often seem to cut more deeply. Recently, a friend called to ask for prayer and direction. Her beautiful, ten-year-old child was trying to deal with negative words spoken to her at school. Some of her classmates were bullying her because her skin tone and hair color are darker than most of her classmates. "You're ugly," one boy yelled, "and you don't know how to dress!" Words can hurt in any medium, but when written they appear a bit less personal. The spoken word is alive. Its power is visceral.[3]

Sound powerfully conveys presence. American Jesuit priest, professor, and religious historian Walter Ong captures this idea in an anecdote he shares about the hunter and the buffalo:

The hunter, remember, can see, touch, smell, and taste a buffalo when the buffalo is inert, even dead. If he hears a buffalo, it's a different matter: the buffalo is doing something. Sound signals the present use of power. Scholars sometimes say that primitive peoples naively associate words with power. It is such scholars who are naïve: if you think of real words, of sounds, words are always an indication of power-in-use.[4]

If that beast is making noise, move out of the way. It's alive! Sound brings something unique to the scene. Movement, action, even living power. Indeed, the power of the spoken word is vastly different from the written or printed images.

With the exception of touch, the power of the human voice to demonstrate affection is unsurpassed. Foremost is the connection between our breath and our beingness. Breath is life. The voice emerges from within an individual reaching out from the breath of one to be received by another. Moreover, voices blend in conversation with more nuance and finer shades than in writing or text message. Although a letter can be very personal and the particular words chosen thoughtfully, poetically, and clearly, writing is external and much more formal. Ong further explains, "even in the physical world this is so. Sounds echo and resonate, provided that reciprocating physical interiors are at hand. Sight may reflect from surfaces."[5]

There is something deep and alluring about the voice. Understanding this aspect of the spoken word as a way of revealing presence makes the Psalmist's words especially meaningful when we read: "Deep calls to deep at the sound of your waterfall; all Your waves and breakers have swept over me" (Psalm 42:7, NASB). The picture of being engulfed in the totality of God echoes through the longings of every human. Longing for God; longing for each other. Longing to hear the presence of each person who is special to us. This is a desire for true fulfillment. Lovers need to be with each other. So do friends and family. When we can't be in each other's presence, we can try to keep the ones we love in our thoughts and our hearts.

The Power of Presence: With-ness

Remembering God's presence in our daily doings and dwelling on Him throughout the day, helps us stay in close communion with Him even though we're not in physical proximity. This practice brings light to the ways our human relationships can be nurtured even when we're apart. Although we can't see God physically, we remember Him, call upon Him, dwell on His goodness, and speak to Him as the day goes on. Like seventeenth-century monk Brother Lawrence learned while doing chores in the monastery, we can "practice the Presence of God" no matter what we're doing in the normal course of the day.[6] He is with us, always.

We need a similar sort of "with-ness" for our spouses and family members throughout the day. Though we may be in different locations, we can bring them to mind. We can say a prayer, send a text, or perhaps just mention, "I was thinking of you today." This simple phrase affirms and cultivates a sense of with-ness. We can be "with" one another in spirit, or "with" one another in a decision about where to go for vacation or what to have for dinner.

But unless we're spending significant time actually sharing the same physical space, our ability to communicate love is greatly hindered. Being with a person "in spirit" doesn't help much if they need a ride to the airport or a dinner companion. Physical presence is always the most powerful.

Touch comes into play when we're together. Taking time for tender, consistent affection is an important aspect of the physical means of communicating. It's part of the way we nurture intimacy, cultivating a depth of relationship that isn't transactional, but mutually giving and receiving. Relationships are built on being with each other (in each other's presence), and intimacy has a better chance of growing when we're fully present.

But being fully present requires a great deal more than just being in the same room. It means attending to others as fully human. Other people aren't just physically present objects or things. There is a kind of holiness or spiritual presence in seeing others as living, God-created, image-bearing persons.[7]

To be fully present to one another is a gift that we can give the ones we love, a gift that doesn't cost a penny, but is surely priceless. To be fully present involves the here and now, not the there and then. It means being immediately present, focusing solely on the other, turning away from distractions.

This type of immediacy has as much to do with attention as it does physicality. Whereas to be with a person means to be proximate, being fully present requires focus. Are we mindful of others? Do we nurture a heart of compassion and kindness toward a friend who may be away and unseen for many months? Do we even think about them when they aren't present? Is your spouse going about her day with assurance that she's loved and known by you? These questions bid us to consider our attitudes and posture toward those we love regardless of whether they are in the next room or miles apart.

In other words, presence can't always be the place where eyes meet, hands touch, and one person meets with another. As Martin Buber, twentieth-century philosopher and author of the now classic book *I and Thou* said, "Presence is not what is evanescent and passes, but what confronts us, waiting and enduring."[8] Inferred in this immediacy of presence is much more than being in physical proximity. It's knowing the real person, reckoning with that person in front of us, not the one we merely imagine him or her to be. Imagining or projecting our vision of who that friend or spouse could be is emotional quicksand. This type of projection shifts the ground of relationship to shaky ground. Without even a hint of relational trouble ahead, you can take a single, imaginary step the wrong way and find yourself drowning in the sloppy, sinister waters of relational ruin. It isn't that envisioning better versions of those we love is unacceptable, but it's easy to get stuck there and forget who that person actually is at the moment. Getting stuck in a future hope or past nostalgia works against relational health. We lose respect and depersonalize our friend or spouse. We love a fictional person, not the real one standing before us. This frequently results when we buy into the cultural narrative of what it means to be a human being, what it means to be successful, and what it means to be in a relationship.

Saturated in the images and ideas of reality TV, advertising campaigns, and social media, we begin to "consider ourselves and others not as persons, but as products—as 'goods,' or in other words, some*thing* rather than some*one*. We size each other up and make deals with a view to our own profit" [italics mine].[9] It's nearly impossible to communicate love and cultivate intimate relationships when we view others as products meant to satisfy us.

No matter how many people we may influence via social media, they will never provide the satisfaction and joy we feel when playing volleyball, ping pong, or riding the waves on boogie boards with our friends. Even chatting over a cup of coffee is more fun than calculating the number of subscribers we have accrued. On the contrary, such obsessive pursuits can make us more anxious, isolated, and unavailable for committed relationships. Still, for many of us it's more comfortable to allow a screen to mediate our social interaction. Do you ever wonder why this is so? There are multiple reasons but let me offer one. Interacting and relating online with others is less worrisome than building genuine relations. We can hide behind a fake name, false information, and perfectly filtered photos of our face and physicality. Also, we fail to see that a screen—no matter the size—is a kind of wall. We may be able to communicate with ease on the virtual plane, but there is a wall between us. It's more difficult to put up walls and be fake when we're regularly around others. The walls that separate us must come down for intimacy and affection to build.

Creatures or Machines?

Agrarian poet and author Wendell Berry once warned that "the next great division of the world will be between people who wish to live as creatures and people who wish to live as machines."[10] We're never more machine-like than when we fail to be fully present to one another. This happens when our attention is channeled through our devices and away from the person before us or when efficiency dictates the character of our interactions. To give and to be prepared to receive the gift of full presence, then, is to honor and celebrate our status as creatures made in God's image.

— **Michael Sacasas**, Executive Director,
Christian Study Center, Gainesville, Florida

Face-to-face contact allows us to experience the full scope of interpersonal communication. Without it, it's difficult to develop the trust necessary to sustain our relationships. As Paul said in his letter to the Philippians, it's "no trouble for me to write the same things to you again" (3:1, NIV), because this truth must be accentuated: We need to be in each other's presence.[11] Without it, the trust needed to cultivate emotional intimacy takes a back seat. Not prioritizing real presence leads to rippling ill effects such as the loss of human touch and many other nonverbal cues, all of which make our attempts to communicate love much less effectively.

Change Is Certain

We regularly exchange the benefits of face-to-face communication with bits and bytes—fragments, phrases, and acronyms rather than full, personal sentences pregnant with feeling and meaning. In many ways, we have become a soundbite society. An example of this is "X" (formerly Twitter). Short, quippy soundbites have a place in enjoyable banter, but they aren't adequate substitution for meaningful conversation. Screen-mediated relationships are convenient, but not a substitute for presence with friends and family. The gift of being able to contact easily our distant friends and family is clear, but technology is never neutral; there is always a give-and-take. To be wise in our use of these media we must remember to ask ourselves, what's the exchange rate? What does the added convenience of these media do to the depth and richness of our relationships?

MIT Professor Sherry Turkle studies the developmental needs of children. In light of the growing and pervasive presence of artificial intelligence (AI), Turkle observed and interviewed middle school students to understand potential effects of AI. She found that "[T]he developmental implications of children taking robots as models are unknown, potentially disastrous. Humans need to be surrounded by human touch, face and voices. Humans need to be brought up by humans."[12] This and other concerns Turkle raises are unsettling as we collectively stand on the cusp of an entirely new way of being in the world. Our relationships won't only be conducted on the run, but we'll give over more and more of our choices to programs and machines that make decisions for us. Robots, AI, and other non-human helpers will undoubtedly prove indispensable in many situations, but we might end up too quickly adopting them without first assessing possible relational losses.

If we don't ask questions and adopt practices that elevate physical presence, as well as all our human faculties, what it means to be fully human and created in the image of God will continue to be denigrated. This isn't a prophetic statement or prediction. We just need to learn from history. Consider the "QR" code technology. It has streamlined purchasing tickets, accessing facts about upcoming events, ordering food in a restaurant, or bypassing a cashier in the supermarket. But has it improved customer service? Who do we contact if we have questions or problems? Where do we go for help? The downside of adopting many digital efficiencies are the frustration and depersonalization they foster.[13]

Human Superpowers

Humans have superpowers. Not like the animated characters in *The Incredibles* or *Spiderman*, but ours are just as extraordinary: namely, we use language to shape our reality. We can think in the abstract and "talk about talking" (metacommunication) to create meaning. Another one of our superpowers is the ability to adapt to change. But change isn't always for the better. Unless we ask tough questions and resist easy change, our sense perceptions quickly adapt and change. Consider this example: How easy is it to bypass connection with family on a holiday because social media keeps us aware of their comings and goings without the need for face-to-face communication? For some—me included—such mediated connection is a Godsend, allowing a sense of closeness to remain when it's impossible to travel. Consider, as well, the ease with which we text a quick hello rather than making a more extended phone call. Consider the reorganizing propensity of earlier tools that have reshaped our perceptions and sense of reality (such as the sense of how long it takes to get somewhere when we shifted from horse and buggies to automobiles), and this is simply the way the human brain works. We create our technologies, and then, in a very true sense, they create us.[14]

Years ago, I studied the influence of mobile phones on interpersonal coherence and relationship development. I wanted to understand better what changes were occurring in the social landscape and what effect the new communication activity might mean for interpersonal communication. I asked students between the ages of 16–29 to take one 24-hour period and refrain (or "fast") from using any of their electronic or digital devices. No mobile phones, no social media, no Internet. Acceptable media choices for the 24-hour period were limited to pen, paper, and books. I didn't give any specific questions but required them to record their perceptions and experiences every few hours in a journal, detailing how they spent their time, and how they felt about it. The results were remarkable.[15] Their responses were so interesting that I spent 15 consecutive years conducting the same experiment.

Over the years student journaling changed, but the most dramatic results involved the one most common response: nearly 90% of the students throughout the years noticed a stark improvement in the quality of their relationships while on their digital fast. Despite the sheer enjoyment and entertainment these digital media gave them, the highest percentage of all participants reported that their phones and computers also served to distract, dilute, and fragment the relationships they considered most important. In many cases, they noted the increased depth of closeness they felt after just one day of giving focused attention to their friends and family and being in their physical presence. My years of study suggest there is a need to prioritize physical presence if we're determined to make and maintain relationships that last.

Although students' negative reports from the fast were negligible, a few were visceral. One response has stayed in my memory from the early years of this research. One student framed his experience as "my day from hell," and went on to say he "freaked out" after just two hours and had to break the fast. Another student wrote: "I hated this and never want to do it again!" Several others who had a rough time in the early part of the day went on to explain a breakthrough experience that began around halfway through the experiment.

But the majority of students told stories of remarkable relational growth. Once they persevered through the initial stages of awkward silence, along with feelings of isolation and frustration, they told encouraging stories of breakthrough. A 20-year-old baseball player expressed a newfound emotional intimacy with his girlfriend: "We've been together for over two years," he said; "I love her, and I thought I knew her, but I never even knew she liked poetry the way I do. We shared so much from our journals that day and got so much closer. It was one of the best times I've ever had with her!" For many students, the initial fear of missing out (FOMO) on fun with friends and family, along with the awkwardness they felt being alone with their thoughts gave way to experiences of freedom, deeper conversation, and clarity through reflection and prayer. My findings suggested a qualitative difference in their relationships as the students spent more time in each other's presence without the distractions of their digital devices. There is power in presence, and rich relational gems to be mined in an environment free of pings, beeps, and other automated alerts.

Conclusion

Along with the student responses, my own studies and my personal life reinforce the difference between being fully present with and exchanging digital messages. Also, we can even spend hours each day near others but not be mentally present. A wandering mind forming mental "to do" lists, lingering in fanciful daydreams, scrolling through newsfeeds, or countless distractions can keep us from being fully present with the ones we love. The difference between being present or distant relationally is the difference between an emotionally rich and poor way of life. It's somewhat akin to the way we so easily confuse the difference between information and knowledge. Information is important; it can lead to knowledge, but information floating on a page isn't the same as having knowledge of that same thing. When information is sought without context or its application, the result is just a mass of information. The same applies to becoming wise. And, as important as it is to be knowledgeable, we can spend so much time boosting our knowledge capital that we forget that knowledge should lead to wisdom.

Participants in my longevity study echoed the questions T. S. Eliot raised in his poetry when he wrote:

Where is the Life we have lost in living?
Where is the wisdom we have lost in knowledge?
Where is the knowledge we have lost in information?[16]

Eliot asks probing and poetic questions. There is power in wisdom, which comes as a result of applying knowledge, i.e., walking it out in everyday life. An example of this is knowing that it's unsafe to drive and text at the same time. We may all know the safety hazards and statistics surrounding this behavior, but if we continue to text and drive, we're clearly not walking (or driving) in wisdom. Knowledge is gained from the seed of information, but unless we do something with it, it lies flat like a cardboard cut-out. So it is with the power of presence. We can be with another in proximity, but far, far away in our minds and hearts at the same time. To be fully present for (and with) the other is an essential way to nurture a relationship.

In this chapter, I've considered the way our voice and physical presence positively affect our ability to flourish relationally. It's not easy prioritizing relationships in a world where physical presence seems less important than it was when there were no smartphones, 24/7 YouTube availability, smart watches, and other high-tech options. I also examined some of the changes taking place in our world that alter the ways we relate to one another. Choosing closeness requires greater intentionality than staying in touch through mediated messaging. It takes more effort and time to make plans for a visit or stop by and knock on your neighbor's door than it does to try and catch up on the run. But relationships on the run can't deeply satisfy our thirsty souls; we need to be with each other in heart, mind, and body.

We have relational choices to make. The desire to pursue intimacy in our relationships requires brave determination to take the road less travelled. Let's continue to explore how the illusions of love hold us back from experiencing love's reality in the next chapter.

Questions for Reflection

1. To what extent do you feel that time you spend with your spouse or friend in-person is valuable? Consider the time spent apart but connected via technology: How is this time different? How is it similar?

2. Explain the difference between hearing words of affection such as "I love you" or "you are the best" as opposed to reading them in a text. Is there a difference? If so, explain.

Chapter 3

Avoiding Relational Fantasies

Love must be sincere. Hate what is evil. Cling to what is good.
— Romans 12:9, NIV

TWENTY DAYS into the COVID–19 pandemic, Jenny was ready to scream. The 2-bedroom condo she and her husband shared with their three kids— all under 7—was beginning to feel like a cage. For the first two or three days of being housebound both she and Jack had done pretty well. Without the morning rush to leave the house by 7:10 a.m., their daily rituals seemed more relaxed and they both felt strangely optimistic about the radical change of pace.

But the COVID–19 honeymoon was over after ten days. Mayhem and destruction had invaded their household and their marriage. The 30-something couple found themselves at odds, trying to navigate the upheaval in their daily life together, along with dealing with the mind-numbing fear about what was happening in the world. Fear. That was the crux of their chaos. Their love, 12 years strong, withered on the vine of unanticipated and relentless worries. In fear of catching the virus, unable to manage the household while working from home with children, their life together quickly unraveled. Marriage vows that burned brightly faded into chaos. They weren't expecting this. Lost in the panic, their marriage ended.

Most of us desperately want to believe in love that lasts but relationships end for a wide variety of reasons, including false expectations. We imagine being in a healthy, long-term, mutually satisfying relationship but we naively base our expectations for it on fantasy and illusions. After all, that's what we see in film, social media, and television.

With all the fanciful stories and unrealistic narratives about love buzzing through the airwaves, is it any wonder so many ask if there is such a thing as a genuine and lasting relationship? Some of the top reasons why our relationships crumble before they ever have a chance to flourish can be attributed to several fallacies. These fallacies hurt our friendships and marriages and keep them from thriving because they are based on an illusion of love instead of the reality of love. Here are several of those fallacies:

- We accept the illusion of perfection.
- We leap past important steps of relationship development.
- We live for tomorrow or yesterday and lose out on the present moment.
- We look for love in all the wrong places.
- We mistake the other for "the one" who will make us whole.

Attaching ourselves to any of these fallacies is sure to work against the promise of long-lasting, vibrant love.

It's important to adjust our expectations and stay alert to illusory thinking, especially when so many of our interactions occur while we're on the run, busily building lives and careers. We'll never be able to anticipate every potential hindrance, but being aware of them is a first step. Awareness allows us to address critical issues and pave the way to full and life-giving relationships.

Learning to love in a resilient way can't really be separated from the love of God. True, lasting love is knit into our Maker's Being; it's the essence of who He is. Greeting those new in the faith, John the disciple, wrote: "Dear Friends, let us love one another, for love comes from God. Everyone who loves has been born of God and knows God. Whoever does not love does not know God, because God is love" (1 John 4:7–8, NIV). Understanding this kind of love is the necessary foundation of our ability to walk in the beauty of long-lasting love, friendship, and close family ties. Such love is much different from the romantic love portrayed in movies.

In this chapter, I uncover some of the illusions surrounding love and relationships manufactured by popular culture. I reveal some of the ways popular culture has over-romanticized love, depicting it as banal, unfulfilling, and even grotesque. I'll also cover several different interpretations of love and consider why communication is so essential in nurturing loving relationships.

Building Strong Foundations

Relationships that flourish don't just happen by waiting for magic to blink them into existence like Barbara Eden did when she starred as a genie in a bottle in the 1970s television series, *I Dream of Jeannie*.[1] Neither do we live in the fantasy world of Harry Potter, whose elder wand and nimbus 2000 helped him overcome impossible situations.[2] It's a fantasy to think that we can maintain strong ties and not be intentional about making them happen. Such relationships require hard but satisfying work.

Anxiety, loneliness, and depression are like the virus faced by the young couple with three children in the introduction of this chapter.[3] Before and after the height of the pandemic, signs of excessive stress showed up in numerous mental health studies.[4] Many still-married couples were unhappy. Hyper-happy relations are Hollywood creations, they aren't reality. We need to understand the divine dimensions of love that have been buried under the weight of popular culture's hold on our collective perception. From there, it's crucial to understand and embrace the characteristics of true love—that is, those elements that are pure, noble, and lovely. These are aspects of love that bear the fruit of the Spirit. They involve goodness, kindness, and gentleness. As we lay hold of these nutritional and delightfully satisfying fruits, we can begin to overcome the fanciful ideas about love that make for a toxic relationship cocktail spilling over into illusory expectations, concocted more of fantasy and false idols.

The Apostle Paul challenges us to dwell on the truth. After charging the young Christians in Philippi to focus their attention on Christ, he tells them: "Finally, brothers and sisters, whatever is true, whatever is noble, whatever is right, whatever is pure, whatever is lovely, whatever is admirable—if anything is excellent or praiseworthy—think about such things" (Phil. 4:8, NIV). As we meditate on these things, the false idols of a so-called perfect relationship are the first to be dashed.

Understanding the different ways love is understood will also help to reduce the gap between your expectations of a healthy marriage or close friendship and the ability to nurture it. Looking at these illusions may be hard, but it helps us to avoid falling into the pit of relationship-destroying lies. Most importantly, to press through the illusions, we need to keep the truth about love in front of us as presented by the Apostle Paul: "Love is patient, love is kind. It does not envy, it does not boast, it is not proud. It is not rude, it is not self-seeking, it is not easily angered, it keeps no record of wrongs. Love does not delight in evil but rejoices with the truth. It always protects, always trusts, always hopes, always perseveres" (1 Cor. 13:4–7, NIV). This love may no longer be regularly practiced in American culture, but it remains true and provides a solid foundation on which to build our relationships. But Paul's "love chapter"—1 Corinthians 13—lays the groundwork and standard for the type of lasting love we're discussing here.

Everywhere, we're inundated with distorted versions of love. We see it displayed openly in popular music and films. In TV shows we learn that friends always work things out; nerdy boys always get the beautiful blond; and a quirky group of scheming co-workers are always there for one another.

By contrast, we're tossed back and forth by the waves of life's relentless uncertainties, double standards, and sudden disappointments. In real life, chance meetings and initial chemistry doesn't always end like the movies. Instead of assuming that an ecstatic high or constant peaceful harmony is the norm in strong relationships, we need an understanding of love that's countercultural, one that stands strong against the wind, steady and willing to press through discomfort or pain. Love that's genuine and lasting doesn't retreat when storm winds blow. It stands fast. Among the many ways the Bible describes such a love is that it endures all things, is patient and kind, does not harbor grudges but forgives, and it's one of the only three things we'll take with us when this earthly life is through: "Three things will last forever—faith, hope, and love—and the greatest of these is love" (1 Cor. 13:13, NLT).

A Mother's Gift

The gift of connection felt even more sacred to me when I lost my mother at a young age. Later in life, as a single woman, the risk of losing this gift again also terrified me. Even now, after years of healing, I sometimes have to face deep feelings of loss when I express love. Despite the uncomfortable fears, I still aspire to have a generous heart. My mother's affectionate bravery, even in the face of death, taught me that love makes life worth living. It's true that if I am to feel connected to a friend, a family member, and especially a partner, it means I have to open myself up to being hurt. Yet, I also get to experience God's most common way to heal the wounds, and one of His greatest gifts on earth—the presence of another.

— **Mary Stucchi**, Photographer, West Palm Beach, Florida

Living out our relationships via screens has created a generation of frictionless contact—people who know how to use digital devices well but may not realize how these tools are depersonalizing our relationships. Charlie Warzel of *The Atlantic* explains this idea: "Our tools take us out of the practice of attentiveness. It's not just that we're distracted, but that our devices offer us the option to attend less to the world around us."[5] This tendency to be distracted with our digital devices along with the super pace of everyday life, creates space for these false notions of love to spread. As we begin to understand the disconnect between our hopes and desires for lasting relationships and our collective experience, we'll have a better chance of making the changes necessary to nurture friendships and romantic love that flourishes.

Love's Illusion in Popular Culture

In many ways, the very idea of lasting love has lost its shine. This is partially due to the reality that our minds and hearts have been significantly shaped by the superficial images and simplistic stories of popular culture rather than the sobering words of Scripture and the challenging teachings of Christ. On TV and in the movies, we see "perfect relationships in which people interact effortlessly . . . our personal communication rarely meets the cultural ideal."[6] Finding the dream man or woman, the perfect friend or parent, is a cause for tears and wasted time. The so-called perfect one does not exist. It's an illusion. The biblical reality is that relationships are difficult.

One reason these illusory ideas surrounding love are so established in our minds is the far-reaching impact of digital media. The goal of drawing eyes to the screen has been standard practice in the entertainment business. The more dramatic the love, the more captivating the story. But illusory notions of love did not start with twenty-first century media. Humans are innate storytellers, and narratives of love have long been with us. Sharing our stories with others is a way to learn from and get to know each other. Jesus taught using story. Stories stay with us and can become "a transformative lens," shaping a path of perception upon which we build expectations and desire.[7]

In recent history, notions of romantic love were played out on the stage through plays and operas. Earlier, dramatic stories were available in novels. Then, as the golden age of radio advanced in the early twentieth century, dramatic storytelling entered America's living rooms, and the commercialization of romance took a giant leap forward. By the mid-twentieth century, the Barbie doll was marketed to little girls. Soon after, her boyfriend, Ken, showed up on store shelves and an entire narrative about their romance emerged. "Love" became more about having the right clothes and accessories than having the right heart. Today, the Barbie fantasy continues with make-up, movies, and video games that market romance as a commodity.

Advertising agencies stoked the public's flames of desire for acceptance and superficial love through glossy campaigns that depicted happy, glamorous people. As the toy industry and its partner in crime, television, rose in influence they delivered false notions of love to 5- and 6-year-old children. Meanwhile, early cartoons such as "Betty Boop" and daytime dramas also had a powerful influence. Glamorous soap stars, rock legend lifestyles, and literary portrayals of romantic ecstasy continue to shape our collective idea of love throughout the twenty-first century. The commercialization of these characters and so many other icons of the media spread illusory ideas of love.[8] From songstress Madonna's music videos to Kim Kardashian's exploitation of her sexual persona through social media, the last 50 years of entertainment media have regularly conflated love and relational satisfaction with sex, celebrity, and power. Today, that false picture of love continues and appears to be even more entrenched. One example is the casual sexual encounter known as a "hook-up," a practice that makes uncommitted, casual sexual interaction acceptable without any promise of marriage—or even relationship.

Although the "no strings attached" behavior isn't a new phenomenon, hook-up culture increased with the availability of the birth control pill and the sexual revolution of the 1960s. There is evidence that hook-ups have slightly decreased among teenagers in the 2020s, but concurrent with this development is the report that "sexual behavior outside of traditional committed romantic pair-bonds has become increasingly typical and socially acceptable."[9] The American Psychological Association reported that both women and men experience negative feelings of guilt and shame from hooking-up. This behavior results in many negative consequences, both for the people involved, and future relationships. Yet one-night stands are glamorized. Hook-ups and one-night stands detract from the reality that relationships require effort and time. Some believe that the word "work" should never be associated with love, while that's true, it's part of the illusion that has been pushed by popular culture.

Total blame for misrepresentation of love does not lie solely at the feet of talented filmmakers; however, such media have had much influence in shaping the narrative called love.[10]

Biblical Love: A Different Story

Romantic love that's wholesome and earned through effort is often treated as naïve or trivial. With few exceptions, mediated stories of enduring, loving commitment are becoming uncommon. Instead, many stories conflate love with horror, heartbreak, fantasy, or a combination of all three; it appears that steadfast love is impossible. The version of love portrayed in popular culture has become more mythical than real, both utopian and dystopian.[11]

The disconnect between the biblical idea of love and your ability to experience love is not simply a result of accepting the numerous false media depictions. We must also confront the internal, emotional reality of our humanness, or what it means to be human. We're broken people, living in a broken world, partly trying to fix ourselves by taking love from other broken souls. Feelings are real, but they can deceive us; falling in love with a feeling is different than loving others. Loving others and being loved is a heartfelt commitment followed with self-sacrificial action.

Finally, the speed and accessibility of distraction feeds the illusions of love. The destructive influence of internet pornography and its easy, one-click home delivery system sets the tone for our collective notion of love as quick sex. When you have experienced genuine love it's easy to see that what's offered through porn and happy hook-ups is hardly more than an elusive copy. But people who have never tasted or seen the beauty of long-lasting, satisfying, love can easily fall for a substitute. It's clear that the definition of true love throughout the years has morphed into something that's far different from the loyal, kind, faithful, patient, and compassionate qualities that form a biblical understanding. As a result of flimsy, cheap depictions of love, the foundations necessary for long-lasting, satisfying relationships have taken a backseat to ideas put forth by our media.

Regardless of this deep media mess about love, blame for our relational brokenness involves many historical factors. Although media misrepresentations mentioned here are a major part, there are other factors to consider.

Further back in history there exists great diversity in expressions and definitions of love. Many of them have long been forgotten or are named something else. For instance, *mania* was used for love that depicts a possessive, dependent type of love that jumps into passionate eros quickly, even recklessly. *Ludus* is a non-committal game-playing version of love, seductive and casual in its attitudes and actions. Although the word is ancient, today's trendy sexual hook-ups and "friends with benefits" provide a contemporary version of *ludus*. Another example is *courtly love* which, although now outdated, involves chivalric or service-oriented love. Being alert to the powerful and persuasive elements of these varied interpretations may help us see more clearly the beauty and reality of the grounded, substantial, self-giving, "true" love depicted by Christ and throughout Scripture.[12]

Despite the sway of popular culture, the more distinctly biblical narratives of love remain true. They are grounded "stories" about how God deals with children who make mistakes or deliberately reject His guidance. Jesus's story of the prodigal son in Luke 15:11–32 is one example of this. It's a parable that tells the tale of a rebellious son who left his father and his family to pursue pleasures and personal gain. While away, this prodigal lost all his father had given him, along with his dignity. When he returned, it wasn't to a scolding parent who punished or chided him. Instead, the father was overjoyed with his son's return and welcomed him back with joyful zeal. That's love.

Love isn't just forgiveness, though it's a major part. God's love is a genuine open heartedness toward the good of the wayward one. It's "believing the best," maintaining a compassionate regard for the one who is lost or confused. That's the way of love, God's love. Here's the thing about it: God's love isn't natural. It's supernatural, something we can't manufacture or do if we just try hard enough. When we truly love each other we want the best for the other person. We're willing to step back, lay down our power, and put their good before our own. In fact, it may be said that loving someone with biblical love often leaves us quite helpless. It's a helpless love.

This is one of the reasons we so easily slide into the illusions of love. Truly loving others is challenging. To love this way, we need more than the natural inclination to simply be with another. We need something supernatural. We need the Lord! As we call upon His power and wisdom to truly love others, we learn more fully to trust in the One who modeled it for us in the sacrificial giving of His Son, Jesus Christ. This supernatural power is the stuff of which true love is made. This love is of Divine origin. It's known as *agape* love. Agape is the Greek word that's sometimes translated as charity but is much more than our contemporary definition infers. Charity is mostly associated with caring for those less privileged or taking up a cause for the sake of the poor or homeless. Charity is more closely akin to altruism in our current vernacular and does not quite express the fullness of the agape love of the New Testament. Agape has a different dimension. It's the deepest expression of God's love for us—a love that occurs in spite of our inability to be consistent. In spite of our failure, our inconsistency, our indifference or defiance, agape loves. Agape love is the gold standard of love for all our relationships. It is God's perfect love. When we love similarly, we can cultivate agapeic love on earth. Although this divine dimension of love can flow over and throughout any of our relationships, intimate or otherwise, our human, flawed love does not guarantee relational flourishing. It's the practice of this divine love that leads to flourishing. When both parties learn to practice agape love, they begin to thrive in real love together.

Agape shows us that if love is to be more than an ideal or unrealizable dream, then it must stay connected to God and also to the earth. In other words, love must be firmly rooted in the reality of ongoing, everyday life. Yet, it must also find its source in a place untouched by the havoc of the unpredictable universe of human emotions and the ups and downs of earthly existence.

The good news is that there is such a place; it's the realm of the human heart, the place through which the river of God's love flows. The river of God's love does not dry up when our feelings fade for others or when adversity comes. But where is that river, and how do we stay current in its lively stream? God's love is its author, its source. In fact, scripture teaches us that God is love. Love is knit into our Maker's Being, the essence of His Being. Understanding and anchoring ourselves into this source of pure agape love is the necessary foundation of our ability to walk in the beauty of long-lasting love and friendship in which we flourish.

Conclusion

In summary, true love, lasting friendship, solid, and flourishing family life requires true, self-giving love. It requires taking a strong look at the cultural fallacies of love we may have taken on. As a reminder, some of the most prominent reasons why our dream relationships die before they ever have a chance to fly involve one or more of the five fallacies.

- We accept the illusion of perfection.
- We leap past important steps of relationship development.
- We live for tomorrow or yesterday and lose out on the present moment.
- We look for love in all the wrong places.
- We mistake the other for "the one" who will make us whole.

Attaching ourselves to any of these fallacies is sure to work against the promise of long-lasting, vibrant relationships.

There is an overarching illusion, however, one that I have not included in the five fallacies above, but one that has gained traction in the last twenty-five years and helps support all others. It's the idea that love is true only "as long as it lasts." Such a temporary, superficial version of love hardly seems worthy of all the attention we give it. Yet this idea has rooted itself in our culture and is becoming a new norm. But true love isn't a patchwork quilt sewn together with countless partners who love for a time and then rip their patch away, leaving a shabby, shredded blanket.

There are many reasons for the proliferation of this illusion. The first has to do with the disintegration and breakdown of our self-as-a-part-of-community, which is a deeply significant aspect of the problem but not the central feature of this book. Another reason may be found in something much more basic, and that's an unwillingness to listen intently and from the heart. Listening is a key piece of the communication process, and central to the flourishing of all relationships. This, along with commitment to communicate regularly and forgive generously, is essential to the growth of our relationships. For this, we must learn to listen to God.

Questions for Reflection

1. Of the five fallacies mentioned in this chapter, which one do you find most challenging to embrace or release?

   - We accept the illusion of perfection.
   - We leap past important steps of relationship development.
   - We live for tomorrow or yesterday and lose out on the present moment.
   - We look for love in all the wrong places.

- We mistake the other for "the one" who will make us whole.

2. Where do you see the illusion of love showing up in our world?

3. What aspects of the divine dimensions of love (agape) do you find most challenging, and which ones do you find resonate most?

Chapter 4

Listening to Love

My dear brothers and sisters, take note of this: Everyone should
be quick to listen, slow to speak and slow to become angry.
— James 1:19, NIV

OUR CHURCH was growing quickly and becoming known throughout the
county as the place to be. My husband and I loved this community and invested ourselves heavily in it. We ministered on the worship team together,
each week joining the pastor on the stage to lead the music. We served as
home group leaders, cultivating community, caring for 20 to 30 others. We
sent our children there for private Christian education. All was well until
the senior pastor began preaching a false gospel that did not match up with
Jesus's own words. Our beloved church was becoming a self-improvement
program that centered around gaining wealth.

The errant messages began with preaching that combined ideas taken
from the discipleship movement of the 1970s (i.e., obey your authorities
or you'll be cursed and die), and the prosperity movement of the 1990s
(i.e., God wants you to have wealth). Scriptures were taken out of context.
On Palm Sunday, the sermon appropriately addressed Jesus's ride into
Jerusalem but gave that entrance into the city a strange twist. The pastor
likened the donkey Jesus used to ride into town to driving a Cadillac or
Mercedes Benz into New York City. He claimed that instead of walking into
Jerusalem, the donkey was a sign of wealth and prestige, an indication that
God intended that kind of luxury for us all. He claimed we should speak
it and seek it, even using relationships with people he called the goats to
line our pockets with wealth, for God's glory. The church's fall into false
teaching was heartbreaking. It still makes me wince. The teaching became
so distorted that we could no longer stand on the stage in good conscience.
We knew we had to leave, but we worried about how it might affect our
children, threaten our precious friendships, and tear up our lives.

We tried to speak to the pastor and then to politely resign, but he
wouldn't accept our resignation. He told us definitively that if we left, we

would be in direct disobedience to God. We tried again to explain our concerns. He didn't listen to us. He already knew what to say, regardless of our heartfelt concerns anchored in Scripture. Finally, we resorted to sending a letter explaining that it was time for us to leave. "I am your pastor," he responded. "You must obey me." So we left quietly. The man was infuriated and responded by sending a letter to the entire congregation to let them know we were leaving in disobedience to God. My husband and I felt betrayed, hurt, and horrified.

Throughout my life I had been taught to listen to pastors and priests as voices of authority, but I also knew that I had to listen to God. I had to learn what it meant to sit in stillness, pondering God's word, waiting upon Him for direction, comfort, and hope. Even after we departed our precious fellowship of believers, the process of letting go of that community took time. In the ensuing months and even years, I gradually worked through the deep disappointment. It took time to arrive at a place of forgiveness. Clarity and healing didn't come quickly. I found myself waking in the middle of the night to pray and seek God's consolation. Listening in solitude and quiet helped me to stand strong. Slowly, I began to learn the discipline of stillness. After many years of practicing stillness, I began to see what it means to truly trust God, even during times of injustice, malice, and church abuse.

Learning to listen to God helps us become better listeners to those we love. In this chapter we'll explore what it means to listen to what's unspoken and address some of the obstacles to listening. First, the heart.

Listening: The Heart of Communication

Listening is the heart of communication. All good and true relationships—with God, others, and even ourselves—are anchored in open-hearted listening. While listening begins with proper auditory function, that's just the start. Our ears allow us to hear another's voice, but unless we're intentional about quieting the external and internal noises, we'll always battle personal distractions.

To listen well, we need to attend to what's being said, then interpret it, and even recall it. Each of these elements is important, but even when we've practiced and are determined to listen more carefully, our communication is blocked by the busyness of our own plans. Professor and author Paul Soukup reminds us that this is what happened to Peter on the Mount of Transfiguration:

Here his communication behavior seems so natural . . . and, on reflection so wrong. He begins describing, planning, speaking almost as if he doesn't know what he's says. And finally, God has to interrupt him to get a word in edgewise. 'This is my Son, the Beloved. Listen to him.'[1]

Listening is active and requires skill, practice, and especially attitude. It requires an open-hearted mindset. We have to enter conversations without being biased toward what the other is saying. This is where our pastor failed us; he required others to agree with him even before he listened to them.

Listening well means attending to what someone else is saying and rightly interpreting its meaning—including what she is feeling. We listened to our pastor's preaching with the truth of Scripture in mind. We rationally compared the two. As my husband and I listened heartfully to each other's concerns about our church, we understood our shared feelings and realized we could no longer stay. Our hearts became one. When we listen from the heart, we're attuned to our emotions.

Undoubtedly, the heart and the mind are intimately connected, but we need both heart and mind to become good listeners. As we listen with the heart, we begin to understand the hopes and feelings that are behind the words of the people we love. First, the heart opens the door to empathic and sympathetic listening for more satisfying relationships. Asking questions about our loved ones is essential: Who is this one that I most adore in my life? How can I make sense of why my father always uses guilt to manipulate me? What did I say to make my spouse shut down? Why do my mother's eyes fill with tears when we disagree?

Questions like these plague us all, but they're important to ask. Only active, empathic listening can help us find answers, and this requires focus. It requires us to avoid the distractions outside of us and within us. There's nothing wrong with a quick text message asking someone how they're doing, but that's not a substitute for attentive listening. When we listen, we're focused on another's meaning. We seek to understand him, not to agree or disagree.

Many of the misunderstandings that occur in our primary relationships can be successfully addressed by learning to listen well. Listening well isn't just a matter of being attentive, or to recall what was said. When we listen empathically, we listen relationally with a goal to comfort, respect, and understand. In one study, two thirds of the respondents said that there was no one in their lives who would truly listen to them—that is, no one who could listen to them without judgement.[2] In spite of all the advanced communication technologies available today, people don't seem to be attending to one another's thoughts and feelings.

Seeing with God's Eyes: The Power of Dialogue

My husband Jon and I recently joined a small group at our church. One of the couples in the group often sit a couple of rows behind us during church. I hadn't noticed them before we met in the small group. Now, I recognize them because I know them. To truly see others, we must first know them; otherwise, their faces blend into the crowd. If we aspire to see others as God does, we must earnestly strive to know him. Father Pedro Arrupe reflects on this in his prayer, which begins:

> Teach me your way of looking at people:
> as you glanced at Peter after his denial,
> as you penetrated the heart of the rich young man
> and the hearts of your disciples.
> I would like to meet you as you really are,
> since your image changes those with whom you
> come into contact.[3]

Jesus knew Peter, the rich young man, and his disciples. Seeing people as Jesus sees them begins by knowing God. This understanding is fostered through genuine dialogue with our Creator. True dialogue necessitates sharing, asking questions, listening attentively, and patiently waiting. It challenges us to consider and be open to perspectives different from our own, recognizing that God's thoughts and ways differ from ours, as Isaiah 55:8 reminds us: "For my thoughts are not your thoughts, neither are your ways my ways" (NIV). As we dialogue with God, we see him, and only then are we able to see others through his eyes.

—**Diane M. Badzinski**, Professor of Communication, Colorado Christian University

Attentive listening helps us to slow down and remember our distinct, God-created humanness. When we truly listen to one another, we defy those who think of us as machine-like, messaging robots. We aren't just senders and receivers. We're God's image bearers who, like Him, can listen to, and for, love. In other words, our ability to listen to God and each other is countercultural, even counter-technological.

Many of our daily interactions take place virtually and from remote locations and human contact is declining. Robots, computerized voice assistants, and artificial intelligence (AI) are creating an environment that's detaching us from ourselves and others. We message wildly, but few of us listen attentively. Over time, our interactions become more like voice mail systems rather than thriving social relationships. Though we long for actual people who will listen to us personally, time spent together becomes increasingly less.

Listening for Community

By contrast, our brains are wired to relate. We're most content when we're relating to God and others. This is how we were created. We're social creatures, created to be with others. Isolation hurts us. Like actor Tom Hanks, who played the FedEx employee stranded on a desert island in the movie *Cast Away*, we'll create our own "Wilson" (which he fashioned from a volleyball) just to maintain the barest sense of companionship. We expect to be heard and understood within a community. We need to know someone is listening, A recorded voice may pass along needed information, but it can't substitute for a human on the other end of the conversation.

How does this need interact with our relationships? Is community really possible? How do we promote a community that sincerely focuses and listens to one another?

Right now, our future as God's image-bearing listeners looks rather grim. Experts in the fields of psychology, sociology, communication, and medicine have concluded that a "new normal" for the American public is on the horizon. It's a way of being in the world that prefers machine-to-human over face-to-face communication. It will be extensive, and "the shift to tele-everything will diminish in-person contact and constrict tech users' real-world support systems and their social connections."[4] Let's look at some examples of why this is so.

During the COVID-19 pandemic, screen time was crucial in helping us stay connected to friends and family across the miles, but it also contributed to one of the most devastating and downward trends in mental health. Researchers reported that more people experienced clinical depression and other anxiety disorders than at any other time in recent history, citing lack of physical contact and loneliness as main culprits.[5] The good news is that these patterns of decline can be turned around once small changes are made in communication habits. One study found "that students who limited their use of Facebook, Instagram, and Snapchat to 30 minutes a day for three weeks had significant reductions in loneliness and depression as compared to a control group that made no changes to their social media diet."[6]

Listening is also impacted negatively by information overload and media saturation. As the amount of information we have increases, stress rises. Mental health declines. We seek professionals to listen to us, partly because no one seems to be listening amidst the noise of everyday life. We're anxious and don't know where to turn.

Researchers are now connecting the plethora of information and diminishment of social interaction with the mental health crisis in America. In a study conducted by the American Psychological Association two thirds of millennials experienced regular symptoms of anxiety.[7] The addictive properties of always available media have bled into every sector of society.[8]

The most negative conclusions related to mental health revolve around something called the Loneliness Index. The UCLA Loneliness Index was originally created to measure college students' experience of loneliness and isolation. It involves a 20-item scale that rates their subjective experience of loneliness.[9] In addition to the expanding array of anxiety disorders, it appears loneliness is rising in what health experts report are epidemic proportions.[10] About 50% of Americans report feeling lonely sometimes often. Moreover, those who never use social media seem to be just as lonely as very heavy users.[11] Increasingly, however, social media is correlated with the rise in loneliness. It's possible that loneliness is simply being measured more accurately in this age of information, but the one steady contributing factor to loneliness appears to be the lessening of face-to-face interaction.[12]

The tentacles of loneliness are far-reaching. It's the reason many people cite for cheating on their marriage partners. In some cases, up to 70% of married couples said they cheated on their spouse because they were lonely or didn't feel understood.[13] The words "She isn't interested in anything I do," or "He doesn't hear a word I say," are common complaints.

So much relational chaos might be avoided if we paid more attention to sharpening our listening skills. In short, real community and relational harmony requires face-to-face listening. We would do well to understand the importance of listening as it relates to empathy and how it contributes to relationships that flourish.

Impediments to Listening

Many obstacles to listening have hindered relationships long before our current cluttered media landscape. Today, however, the ability to be a good listener is made more difficult by the information glut.

The umbrella term that covers all the stimuli that interferes with listening is called noise. The human brain, however, has an amazing ability to filter and focus. Even in a loud, crowded room we can engage in an intense one-on-one conversation. Similarly, we can tune out the noise of screens in restaurants, waiting rooms, and hospital rooms. Even more importantly, we can listen despite the distractions caused by our digital devices. We have the capacity to stay focused even as our lives become busier and noisier. Since we can overcome the noise, we need to understand the things that cause the noise, so that we may facilitate better relationships. Three overlapping categories make it difficult to focus and listen: 1) distractions, 2) frictionless interaction, and 3) self-focus.[14]

Distractions

Distractions are like weeds. Most of them are hard to pull up and they grow much more profusely than the cherished orchid you've been nurturing for months. Weeds may be pretty, but they don't belong in the garden. Mexican Violets, for example, are beautiful, but they can overwhelm a garden and completely obscure everything else that's been planted.

Like weeds, beeping alerts that intrude from our personal mobile devices are often distractions—part of the overwhelming amount of input we receive incessantly from our digital devices. Many of the sounds and images interrupting our days require no immediate response. But combined, they become part of a vast glut of information that surrounds us, bidding us to check, look, and respond even when we're in the middle of doing something else.

The weight of these distractions causes stress that weaves itself through our conversations with friends and family and interrupts our ability to give focused attention and real listening. Giving partial attention can become so normal that it seems natural, even invisible. But continued partial attention is pitiful; it takes the wind out of the sails of our friendships.[15] This is what easily happens when we conduct our relationships almost solely on the run. Over time the very life of our friendships can dwindle and before we know it, they become diluted into something superficial. When friends keep their eyes glued to a digital device, we feel like media distractions are more important to them than we are.

To sustain these relationships, we need a break from the noise. No matter how much fun or calming it might be to endlessly scroll, it takes time and focus away from the ones we care about most. To conduct a real, listening-intense conversation, we might have to go to a coffee shop rather than a sports bar. Or we might have to agree to turn off our phones before sitting down for a chat. We might even have to go for a walk on the beach, in the woods, away from city life.

Frictionless Interaction

Conflict might be the first synonym that comes to mind when we hear the word friction. However, friction in "frictionless interaction" doesn't infer a rift or irritation with another person. Rather, frictionless refers to the lack of in-person social interaction people need to make room for each other's differences. This type of noise involves what happens when too many of our conversations take place via digital messaging. The immediacy of a digital exchange can be fun, but it also establishes a frictionless environment, one that misses the nonverbal factors that contribute so widely to the communication process. The more our interactions occur online, the less time we seem to take to analyze and discern what's being said. We're far less likely to say silly and even offensive things when we're sitting in the same room with others. Consequently, we're more likely to listen to others when we communicate in face-to-face settings.

Digital devices allow us to quickly make plans or accomplish tasks. Making plans while on the run is another way that face-to-face connection is minimized. To react speedily to a digital message reduces the likelihood that we'll consider what was written and reflect on it. We remove the tension that typically takes place when we share physical space.

A proverb that reminds us of the importance of real social interaction is often quoted when thinking about the need for face-to-face communication: "As iron sharpens iron, so one person sharpens another" (Prov. 27:17, NIV). Without face-to-face social interaction, we miss so much. It's all too easy to jump into a digital conversation with our gut, which doesn't give enough time to truly understand who the other person is, or what he is saying. We all know how easy it is to participate in or point out the major misunderstandings that take place online, but the relational fallout from these misunderstandings is an important reminder not to engage with our gut. Ironically, frictionless messaging produces a different kind of friction, namely, conflict, generated by misunderstanding. Communicating online or via text can soon resemble a boxing match.

Self-focus

Beyond these external obstacles to listening, there are internal reasons why people don't listen that we need to understand. These come under the umbrella of self-focus. We can't listen well when we're thinking about ourselves, how we're feeling, or what we're going to say next. Such self-absorption may be more challenging for those raised in an individualistic culture than a collectivist one.

There are reasons we become self-focused. Many are understandable: personality, external stressors such as work or sickness, interior unrest or confusion, lack of clarity, and numerous other factors. All of these factors come into play to affect our ability to adjust or maintain the level of focus necessary to really listen to another. From time to time, my husband and I still wonder why our pastor was so self-focused in his discussions with us about the direction of his preaching. Was he fearful of failing? Was he captivated by the recent church growth? Sometimes I think he confused his role as pastor too closely with his personal identity. Or maybe it was his vision of the surrounding community that he referenced every Sunday. To this day we still don't understand why he refused to listen to our concerns. But we learned much from walking through that misery. Entrenched self-focus and unwillingness to listen may be difficult to change, but these impediments to listening must be faced and addressed if we're to maintain and strengthen fruitful relationships.

Listening to the Unspoken

Silence, or being ghosted, can cut like a knife. When someone has been wronged in a relationship and the other refuses to discuss his culpability, communication shuts down. Hardly anything hurts us more than when a loved one gives us the silent treatment. But other than this harsh use of silence, there are times when silence is necessary to support the relationship, particularly as silence is such a necessary part of the process of listening. When used properly— for example, as a respectful way to consider more carefully the thoughts or accusations of others—silence can nurture relational communication. In fact, it can even work miracles in a relationship if it's used carefully to really consider what the other is saying.

Silence can give us the mental and heartfelt space to hear what's unspoken; to sense nonverbally how others feel about what they are saying. The silence of a pause may also be a blessing to our loved ones who are processors, or people who like to ponder and take a few moments to consider their response. In these cases, we should prepare our hearts before entering into dialogue.

It's difficult to remain quiet, or to listen thoroughly, while your friend, spouse, or child is speaking. This is especially true when we have strong feelings about the subject being discussed. When we remain silent after they've finished speaking, it can feel like a betrayal or a shirking of our responsibilities to respond. Instead of immediately responding with our gut (or heart), we should simply say, "Let me carefully consider what you've said." And then we should, indeed, carefully consider it on our own before responding in full. This is where regular intervals of personal, silent meditation and the discipline of solitude can become a way to prepare ourselves for the tough times that every friendship, marriage, and family will encounter. Spending time in silent solitude with yourself and the Lord isn't just a practice for monks. Christian author and Anglican priest David Runcorn suggests solitude is a necessary means of detachment from the world and explains its connection with our ability to truly love one another:

> Detachment enables us to stand back. It enables us to gain a wider perspective. It is not the withdrawal of love and involvement, but a more careful and discerning offering of it. Without detachment a sensitive love for this world, in all its complexity and pain, will be overwhelmed and drained empty.[16]

This sort of detachment isn't apathy. Learning to give space is precisely how silence may be used as a healing salve to bind up the wounds of too much talk or words that have been said in haste. Advocating complete silence isn't the aim, nor do we want to engage in a type of silence that shuts down and ignores the other. But there are healing properties found in implementing periods of silence—ways that can create space for relational growth. Listening in silent, active anticipation of the other's words is a gift we can bring to the ones we love. Solitude, or a quiet personal space, is often essential for reflecting on a relational challenge. The quiet of our own soul before the face of God can help us address a recurring problem in our own communication style.

The regular practice of solitude can help us hear our loved one's cry to be heard and understood by us. One of the most eye-opening statements in the Bible comes from the pen of Jesus's disciple, John the Beloved, when he heard the voice of the Lord on the Isle of Patmos. John, also known as the Revelator, surely learned about solitude while he was in exile there. The Lord spoke many words to him about each of the young churches and sealed each one with the statement: "He who has ears to hear let him hear what the Spirit is saying to the churches" (Rev. 2:7, AMP). "Ears to hear" are those that truly hear and understand. They help us to overcome the noise of technologies and even our inner voices; to discover our own complacency and character faults. Our wayward pastor I introduced at the beginning of this chapter seemed to lack the ears to hear. So we tried to be his biblical ears for him, in love. In the end, we had to silence his voice in our lives. It hurt. And still does.

Listening for Life

In Isaiah 55:3 we read: "Give ear and come to me; listen that you may live" (NIV). Our listening is one way the Holy Spirit opens our hearts and minds to real life in Christ. In fact, it would be wise to ask these questions of ourselves every day:

- Do I have ears to hear what the Spirit is saying?
- Do I have ears to hear what my child is saying?
- Do I have ears to hear what my counselor is saying?
- Do I have ears to hear what my best friend or loved one is saying?

We need the physical ability to hear, but we also need an attitude that's open to the other with a heart to understand. Deep listening is about attitude, not auditory function. It's about our hearts, especially our deepest feelings and desires. Once we've truly heard God and others, we may be more willing to let God and others hear us; to disclose the hidden secrets of our heart.

Conclusion

Listening takes time and heart. We begin by practicing listening with our heart, becoming more intentional about listening, and listening for the unspoken amid all the noise and distractions. We put ourselves in another's shoes, asking ourselves what it would be like to walk in her life's experiences. We notice the nonverbal messages our friends and family are expressing.

When deep listening becomes a regular part of our lives, we can look forward to lively, open conversations and finding new and expansive places in our relationships. And, with regular doses of solitude introduced into our days, we may find our hearts and minds dwelling more centrally on God's view of our friends, spouses, or other loved ones. Instead of seeing them primarily in light of what they might bring to us, we begin to see each of them through the eyes of the Lord as a unique, gifted, child of God. Listening is much more than gaining a few new tools to add to our communication toolkit. The art of listening is a gift that can help each of us get ready for the joy and refreshment of life-long relationships. In the next chapter we look at the importance of growing in the art of conversation.

Questions for Reflection

1. Noise gets in the way of many of our best efforts to listen well. Which of the three categories of obstacles—distractions, frictionless interaction, and self-focus—that compromise our listening skills do you struggle with most?

2. Working to improve our listening skills is one of the keys to improving our relationships. Explain one or more ways that listening can bring our relationships from chaos to closeness.

3. Write a short paragraph describing how you feel when you are accused of not listening, or how you feel when you become aware that another is clearly not listening to you.

Chapter 5

Speaking Conversationally

Let your conversation be seasoned, as it were, with salt, communicating grace.

— Colossians 4:6, NIV

YOU'VE GONE to the movies together, taken bike rides, and spent hours messaging, but you still don't feel as though you know him well enough to make a long-term commitment. Yet, the more time you spend together, the more you long to get to know this man. Why can't you get into a deeper conversation? Sometimes you feel as though you must pry his emotions out of him. Or maybe it's the other way around? Perhaps she is reticent and guarded. Perhaps you're already married. You'd like to learn more about what makes him tick, but he is overly cautious about disclosing his private thoughts. Maybe it's a friend you enjoy spending time with—gaming, surfing, hiking, or shopping. Again, your conversations never seem to go much deeper than the activity at hand. What can you do to gain more emotional intimacy?

You aren't alone. Many fine relationships struggle with more intimate communication. In forty years of research and relationship coaching, I have heard the same thing repeatedly: "We just don't communicate well," or "Why won't he talk to me!?!" The reasons are many. The answers, however, are often simpler than we might imagine. Learning how to listen with an open mind and with mutuality in mind is a good starting place.

In this chapter, we'll start with the way our digital media environment both opens us up and closes us off to conversation, and we'll address the steady changes in our communication environment. From small talk and texting to intense conversations that flow well, we'll examine what it means to share personal thoughts and feelings. We'll address the tensions involved in self-disclosure and underscore practices that bring God's grace in our conversations. We'll look at how to address the tensions involved in self-disclosure and underscore best practices that bring God's grace into that space.

Why Converse?

We can find it difficult to carry on a conversation that goes beyond the surface, but conversation doesn't have to be superficial chit chat. We need a much richer and more spacious view of conversation. It can be terribly unfulfilling to remain in a relationship that doesn't go any further than "ankle deep."

Living by the Atlantic Ocean in Florida, I've had the blessing and benefit of enjoying the salty air, refreshing sea breezes, and gorgeous blue vistas. But the vastness of the ocean can also be intimidating, even scary. The desire to dive into the deep waters and make a splash is part of the fun of swimming and other water sports. So it is with jumping into deep conversations: scary but satisfying and fun. Without meaningful conversation, a once-lively relationship can dry up and grow stale. In keeping with the sports metaphor, it may feel a bit like being a third-string professional player, thoroughly committed to daily practice but never getting on the field. Constant and loyal, you sit in the dugout for every game. A very invested observer, but just an observer.

Communication isn't the cure for all relational problems, but if you long for greater emotional intimacy with your loved one, or deeper emotional closeness with friends, growing in conversational skills—especially self-disclosure—will be helpful.

There are legitimate reasons that block the flow of conversation, some of which have nothing at all to do with whether you are an interesting person or if you are valued by another.[1] Many of us have not been raised in a conversational environment. Going back as far as the fifteenth century, children have been admonished to be "seen and not heard."[2] We teach youngsters to be quiet when adults are speaking, and there is a time to listen, learn manners, and keep from interrupting. But it's not easy to become a stimulating conversationalist if your words have been stifled in the developmental years of childhood. Some cultures teach people to be quiet, even as an adult; they see talking during meals or asking questions as rude.

Digital devices are leading many children and adults to avoid in-person conversation altogether. Even without using our digital tools, we wear masks that hide who we are, protecting ourselves from potential hurt or misunderstanding. When we remove our masks, we make room for closer relationships. Conversation becomes a joy. Self-disclosure is an important part of conversational magic.

Dwindling Self-Disclosure

Deep conversation often involves a bit of risk. It doesn't always feel safe to share personal feelings, experiences, and opinions. Sometimes there are mental blockages that keep us from even trying. Learning when and how to share personal information about ourselves is quite like learning a language. It emerges from our speech community. When healthy self-disclosure isn't modeled or when the computer, television, and other media are used as substitutes for human interaction, children fail to learn how to have conversations.

This is partially what occurred in the late 1940s, when television entered into the living rooms of the American public. People were mesmerized. Families began sitting in front of the television screen for hours. By the 1960s, when approximately 95% of Americans owned a television set, Baby Boomers had learned to sit passively, watching their favorite shows. Political Scientist Robert Putnam correlates the arrival of television with a decline in social interaction and civic mindedness in his seminal work *Bowling Alone*.[3] Why go out for conversation with friends and neighbors when you could just be entertained by the television screen?

Gen Xers and Millennials followed suit, typically opting for smaller, more portable screens like smartphones, wearables, laptop computers, and tablets. Gen Z, children born after 2000, are true digital natives; they've only known an environment of digital dominance. No matter the generational category, the art of conversation isn't easily practiced while staring at a screen, despite its weight or dimensions. As with any other type of practice, conversation is bound to become less awkward and more comfortable as it's steadily practiced.

Along with the lack of experience with self-disclosure, "Life on the Screen," as MIT Professor Sherry Turkle calls it, is impersonal and reduces our human capacity for empathy. Communicating through screens isn't an adequate substitute for conversation.[4] One example is the impersonal messaging system we call texting. In one way, it's much easier to text a message to a loved one. Rather than speaking face-to-face, texting lowers the intimidation factor. But how does it feel if a boyfriend or girlfriend breaks up with you via text? Or if a friend texts that she's got to take a break from the daily coffee chats you've shared for the last five years? Can a marriage proposal via text really be taken seriously? Emojis and memes may be helpful to infer sadness, anger, or disappointment, but none of these communication devices leave much room for respectful, mature self-disclosure.

Breakups are bound to hurt no matter what the medium, but texting impedes conversation and is the quickest way to hurt someone's feelings. Seen this way, it makes sense that talking about movies and television, the weather, sports, anything but what's in one's heart, is safer and more comfortable. The tendency to hide behind a text or a post is common, but there are ways to take risks that result in positive outcomes, if we're willing to try.

Taking Risks

To move forward and boldly take the necessary risks that allow us to become stronger conversationalists, we might first converse with the One who made us. He knows who we are, behind our masks. He values us as His children. He loves us unconditionally. What a terrific, risk-free conversational partner!

In his second letter to the Corinthian Christians of the first century, Paul the Apostle is clear that if anyone is in Christ, they are a new creature in Christ: "Therefore, if anyone is in Christ, the new creation has come. The old has gone, the new is here" (2 Cor. 5:17, NIV). Such risk-free formation is laced throughout Scripture. Our God's willingness to teach us is evident throughout Scripture. In Paul's letter to the Romans, the message is clear: "Do not conform to the pattern of this world but be transformed by the renewing of your mind" (Rom. 12:2a, NIV).

Once we have asked God for help, we might examine our conscience and ask ourselves: Why am I stuck living on the surface in this relationship? Is there a leftover hurt from a past betrayal of trust, a hurt that never healed? Perhaps a friend mocked you for disclosing personal weakness or you were bullied at school. If getting more personal in conversations has ever ended in disaster, resistance to letting it happen again can be high.

Countless stories, dramas, and songs have been written about such vulnerability. Hip-hop, country, even classic rock songs have much to say on the subject. One classic song from Simon and Garfunkel does more than hint at our struggles to communicate. The song "I Am a Rock" is one that portrays a brave soul who thinks he doesn't need friendship or love. Simon and Garfunkel sing about the walls built around the brave soul's heart as a badge of honor. Listing all the reasons for the wall, the singers let us know how this brave soul cloaks himself with poetry and books to protect himself. The song makes it clear that there is potential pain involved in letting someone get close. The lyrics to this classic tune are worth exploring.[5]

We may not be able to articulate our vulnerability, but we sure can feel it. Risking our heart in relationships is a serious venture, not only because the possibility of betrayal by someone making our personal thoughts public on social media is so real, but also because rejection seems to lurk behind every conversation. Moving from self-disclosure with a loving God to self-disclosure with broken people isn't easy.

Dealing with Embarrassment and Shame

The risk of being hurt isn't the only reason we might avoid self-disclosure. For some families, self-disclosure is shameful, seemingly self-indulgent or egocentric. Different subcultures and geographic regions perceive such personal disclosure as shameful or rude.

Some of us grew up in households where sharing any family information was considered "airing dirty laundry." Such is the case in Jen and Judy's friendship. They went through school together and ran in the same circle of friends. When they got accepted at the same college, they decided to room together and soon became best friends. Both young women were so happy to have found a friend in each other. Halfway into the first semester Judy learned about self-disclosure in her psychology course and began sharing some of her feelings about her parents' dysfunctional behavior. Every time she shared something about her unresolved feelings, Jen withdrew from the conversation. She didn't want to hear about the dysfunction in her best friend's family. Listening to it made her think about the abuse she suffered as a small child, had buried, and tried so hard to forget. She always felt unsafe in her own house until she turned ten, when her father abruptly moved out. Jen's means of coping was to bury it deeply within the subconscious levels of her mind. Before the end of the semester their friendship ended, and they each found new roommates for sophomore year. Neither were sure what went wrong, and didn't bother to discuss it. After the loss of that friendship, Judy was reluctant to disclose anything personal about herself or her family.

Embarrassment and shame are challenging companions to take with us on the road to forming relationships. Even so, we must move beyond cultural barriers and family expectations and move toward greater openness. For as self-disclosure becomes a regular practice, our closest relationships will build strength and find the gentle push into deeper relational waters. Much like speech-making, the more we step out of our comfort zone, the more we build confidence. In a similar manner, the more comfortable we become enjoying mutual sharing and openness, the more our conversational competence will grow, and the relationships we value will have greater opportunity to deepen. The good news is that anxiety over conversation decreases the more we practice self-disclosure.

This is especially true today, when so much of social identity is mediated through screens and at a distance. The probability of flourishing in our close relationships increases with regular, hearty, authentic conversations. The current lack of true openness undoubtedly leads to a sense of insecurity in us. Online "flame wars" are just one way we experience the unfriending, shaming, and ghosting that makes us even more hesitant to share. Many feel as though they are spinning into a self-defeating cycle of relational failure when a promising friendship or possible date leads nowhere fast. After the initial steps of meeting in-person, and experiencing the interest and chemistry, the would-be relationship dissolves for lack of follow through or aversion to risk. We slip back online to safety.

The good news is that the conversational tools necessary to build relationships are available to all of us. We begin with awareness of the need for openness, continue with learning what's appropriate self-disclosure, and move to deepening levels of self-disclosure. Our resulting relationships have greater potential to flourish and are maintained by regular interpersonal communication. We see friends and family learning how to be transparent with one another, and such relationships work, last, and impact every aspect of our lives. Jon Durham-Peters, in his book *Speaking into the Air*, describes self-disclosure as a way of "making space in the world for one another."[6] This doesn't refer to a geographic or physical place; it's emotional space.

Creating Emotional Space

Every fruitful relationship includes both physical space for interaction and the intangible emotional space for relationship. Self-disclosure is key to creating this heartfelt, emotional space for each other. It takes time, effort, and trust.

By opening up and sharing information about ourselves, we invite others in, giving them access to our lives along with an opportunity for reciprocation. This willingness to open up is much more difficult for some people than others. We may think that those who find it easy to reveal personal information are exceptionally confident people, and those who are hesitant are shy or lack self-esteem. These stereotypical ideas of the way people share are only partially accurate. Some find it easier to speak nonstop about themselves but give little space for others to share. Others, more hesitant in disclosing their thoughts and feelings, may simply feel more comfortable waiting for others to reveal personal information. Either way, engaging in open, honest conversation that includes discussing our feelings helps to build trust—the trust necessary for intimacy to bloom and close relationships to remain intact and flourishing. More self-disclosure, however, isn't always better.

Relational conversation doesn't mandate that we reveal every slight personal opinion or feeling to others, what some refer to as TMI, or "too much information." There are times when sharing too much information is inappropriate or overbearing. Also, there are times when we'll need to nod quietly and just listen. Turkle says, "conversations of discovery tend to have long silences."[7] Self-disclosure has different dimensions. We may be quite comfortable sharing a wide breadth of personal subjects with one person, but not inclined to self-disclose at a deeper level. Neither is it appropriate to self-disclose to everyone. Sharing personal information about ourselves is most important with those whom we're emotionally close.

There is also the matter of holding back or concealing information, even if we're speaking with a close friend or neighbor. In some cases, concealment may be just as effective as revealing what's personal. By this I don't mean keeping important information from the other person. Concealment isn't deception. It involves the need to manage opposite but simultaneous psychological needs. An example of this is the internal tension involved in needing personal space while at the same time wanting to spend time with a friend or spouse.

Another of the too-much versus too-little conversation is the on-going need for both openness and concealment in self-disclosure.[8] Although at the time he was discussing some of the ways to maintain a more civil society, professor and cultural critic Neil Postman suggested that "concealment is one of the important functions of language, and on no account should it be dismissed categorically."[9] Although it may seem counterintuitive, this is especially true of our closest personal relationships. Withholding or limiting an impression or opinion of another isn't the same as lying or manipulating someone's true feelings. Not everything is appropriate. When it comes to the act of revealing truly personal information, the stakes are even higher. Our disclosure must be tempered. This is the push and pull, or dialectical tension, that exists in self-disclosure. We want to reveal, but we also want to conceal. There is tension in holding both needs simultaneously.

Many of us in the West don't think twice about blurting out feelings in public or making a spectacle of ourselves online. We seem so committed to being true to ourselves, but when we mistake our "self" for our immediate feelings (which can change, and readily do!), we can too easily end up sabotaging our friendships and other important relationships instead of nurturing them. Treating our feelings as the gauge for what must be shared with another is a set-up for a relational roller coaster. This attitude does not contribute to healthy relationships with our neighbors. Sometimes it's best just to be quiet. This is a matter of being decent and well-mannered. This brings us to the importance of civility and truth.

As much as a return to greater civility in our everyday interactions is important, making concealment our norm isn't conducive to healthy relationships. The tension involved is a necessary one, particularly if we're to maintain civil conversation in the household, the neighborhood, in our friendships, or in the workplace. Holding back our opinions or feelings for a later, more appropriate time is completely within the range of best communication practices, but it requires deep wisdom and a self-awareness. Writing on civility and the importance of maintaining this tension, Postman emphasized the importance of restraint:

> Civility requires not that we deny our feelings, only that we keep them to ourselves when they are not relevant to the situation at hand. Contrary to what many people believe, Freud does not teach us that we are 'better off' when we express our deepest feelings. He teaches exactly the opposite: that civilization is impossible without inhibition. . . . Silence, reticence, restraint, [sic, can be necessary] for people to work together harmoniously.[10]

Self-disclosing, Not Self-focusing

The strength of Americans' "can do" attitude is well known. Many flock to the U.S. in hopes of finding the independence we often take for granted. Yet, we can be so committed to our personal freedoms that we mistake our own opinions for truth. Whether conversing personally or in the public square, the problem is that feelings may change more quickly than the weather. This self-centered way of being doesn't make for healthy relationships in any area of life. Concealment, or limiting self-disclosure, is an appropriate choice in many instances.

The opposite of necessary concealment is over-sharing or TMI. This problematic practice has become trendy. But using social media to share every intimate moment of our lives degrades the importance of self-disclosure. Those who are typically the first to know of a change in their best friend's marital status suddenly find the gory details of the friend's pending divorce posted on social media instead of discovering it in a private conversation. The sacred space of friendship too easily becomes diluted as private subjects become common knowledge. Worse, perhaps, are those who post every inch of their pregnant bellies or details of their weight loss. They turn private matters into public disclosures.

Excessive sharing of every nuance of our life translates into simple emotionalism. Professor Laura Smit captures this outlook:

> We live in a tell-all society, and we tend to assume that our romantic relationships must be founded on complete self-disclosure—not a self-disclosure taking place slowly, over time, or at least over the length of the courtship, but an immediate self-disclosure that holds nothing back from the first date onward.[11]

Complete conversational openness may not be desirable or possible in every close relationship, but it's beneficial when we build mutual trust and respect.

Small Talk

Of course, not all conversation is in-depth or emotionally intimate. Much of interpersonal communication isn't even relationship talk but routine communication, the stuff of everyday life. Such small talk is still essential for building quality in relationships. Communication scholars Julia Wood and Steve Duck suggest that the very character of our relationships "is established primarily by routine, ordinary communication that, over time, shaped it into what it is."[12] Everyday conversation is the very fiber of a relationship. Julia Wood suggests that regular, daily communication is essential and particularly important to the maintenance and growth of relational intimacy.[13]

Interest in another's story, listening well, and engaging in conversation can help free us from self-absorption, an all too common experience of being human. Such conversational skills are a virtue.[14] Instead of concentrating on what's happening in our own life, conversation allows us to discover what's happening in a friend's life. Conversation requires us to think beyond our own concerns. Conversation can help deliver us from the temptation of being overly self-centered.

While conversation alone can't undo our natural tendency to see the world self-centeredly, it's an important step on the path to self-discovery and relational health. Kathleen Norris, author of *Dakota* and essayist on the monastic life, says that conversation frees us from "the presumption of coming to this table [of fellowship] for solace only, and not for strength, for pardon only, and not for renewal."[15] Conversation can help set the tone for relational mutuality. Without mutuality a relationship is one-sided. This is no fun at all and doesn't contribute to the establishment of long-term relationships that thrive.

Conversational Flow

Many people shy away from deep conversations because it can become awkward. When words dry up and there's nothing left to say, the empty space that hangs in the air can be quite uncomfortable. But as anyone knows who has observed others in a dazzling, melodic conversation, a great conversation can be electric. Its dynamism is obvious, even from afar. Such a conversational ebb and flow isn't magical but inexplicable, even mysterious.

Relational chemistry, timing, and the free exchange of ideas, feelings, dreams, and desires help to create flow. Multiple elements help maintain this flow, but one main ingredient stands out: mutuality. A good conversation isn't a monologue. One person can't dominate. Mutuality involves recognizing and respecting others' voices. The art of conversation is like a flowing river; its freshness carries along everything in its current. Remaining curious and interested in the other is a great start.

Team "We"

If you've ever played or watched team sports you recognize when the players' actions sync. The beauty of coordination, of individuals each contributing their gifts, is what makes the team successful. But when players lose sight of the "we" in the team, communication fractures and individual striving, sometimes at odds with each other, enters.

To be in a relationship challenges us to let go of me and mine. It's not that we don't have individual interests and gifts, but that the goal is a stronger team. Sacrifice may be needed for a season in service of "us." Christian relationships redefine what our team looks like. We're siblings of Christ living together before the face of God, seeking together the win of his glory.

— **Annalee R. Ward**, Professor of Communication, Dubuque University

Without a deep sense of the importance of mutuality, the flow of conversation gets stopped up. Mutuality includes giving relational support and empathy. It remembers the "we" instead of "just me."

The opposite of mutuality is one-sided discourse. We might offer much but receive little in return; we don't get to know the person. Similarly, we might hear a lot about someone else, but rarely get an opportunity to share our story. A growing relationship requires giving and receiving, a mutual give-and-take.

Conversational give-and-take reminds us that we're not alone; that being in this world means being with others. We need others to help us know ourselves better, and vice versa. Conversation is a gift, best received and enjoyed with others. Conversation embodies our relationships. Quaker poet and professor Parker Palmer says it well: "The act of knowing is an act of love, the act of entering and embracing the reality of the other of allowing the other to enter and embrace our own."[16]

As we become more comfortable and secure in the art of conversation, letting others know who we are at our core becomes somewhat easier. Self-disclosure becomes more natural. When these skills work together, they can open a relationship to greater fullness and satisfaction. Like a rose in full bloom, the beauty of it is stunning.

Conclusion

To know another person and love them well is something that doesn't collect a paycheck, gain recognition for yourself, or establish a person as worthy and valuable. Yet, it does produce joy and purpose. It's a noble pursuit. Knowing others beyond superficial knowledge also helps us know ourselves better. Deep knowing helps us make sense of life and stay balanced in an unbalanced world. Plunge in. Take chances in conversation. Don't hold back. Love is worth the risk. Self-disclosure with God and others is one of the greatest blessings in life.

Together we've looked at several of the most important building blocks of conversation: self-disclosure, conversational flow, and the need to respectfully approach each other with appropriate boundaries. Each is a key element in the long road to lasting, loving relationships. We also need affection. So how do our bodies figure into this mix? What about the need for affection? More answers to come on this question in the next chapter.

Questions for Reflection

1. Which of the key components to conversation (self-disclosure, conversational flow) do you have the most trouble with and why?

2. What part of the revealing and concealing dialectic feels more complicated for you? Spend a few moments thinking about this and consider why you feel this way.

3. Take a mental trip back to the days when conversation started to feel difficult. Remind yourself what was happening and how you felt during that time.

Chapter 6

Discovering Paths Toward Intimacy

Greet one another with a holy kiss.
— 2 Corinthians 13:12b, NIV[1]

PUPPY LOVE. That's what they called it when I was a teenager. Mom said, "everybody goes through these young crushes, Steph." But I just knew my high school sweetheart and I were different. We were more than just a passing crush. We were fascinated with each other and spent every possible moment outside of school and his football practice together. He made me feel safe. And not just because he was so strong and grown up, but because we both felt much more mature than our age and barely knew what to do with our feelings. We'd spend endless hours at the park, sharing our thoughts and dreams for the future. For the first time in my life, I felt seen, safe, and known. I had never experienced such emotional intimacy.

On cold winter days when he didn't have practice, I'd skip the school bus and he'd walk me three-quarters of the way home, careful to stop several blocks before my street. Then we'd spend an hour kissing under the maple tree on the corner. We even talked about running away to another country and getting married at 18. We worried about how angry our families would be and then giggled as we invoked Romeo and Juliet, spending time fantasizing about what it could be like chasing each other's hearts for the rest of our lives. Oh, there were plenty of romantic delusions and I had crushes before, but this one was different. Soon the sparks in our eyes turned into flaming fires. I didn't know what hit me.

One day when I was cheering him on from the varsity field bleachers, a voice behind me seemed to be cheering just as loudly. I turned and looked at her and smiled, thinking she was just one of my boyfriend's many football fans. She smiled wryly back, looked me squarely in the eyes, and shouted, "He's part mine, too, you know." I shook my head, pushed my shoulders back, and said confidently, "Uh, I don't think so." After the scrimmage our exchange quickly moved to a bit of a scene under the bleachers, ending abruptly when she flung the final barb: "I give him what you won't, *and he loves it!*"

Gut-punched

That's the tale of my first love. I wanted to wait until marriage for sexual intercourse, but she was willing to use that powerful desire to put a wedge between my boyfriend and me. He denied her claim but how could she know that my boyfriend and I hadn't gone all the way unless he had told her? Trust was broken. I no longer felt safe. Although I was still completely in love with him, I broke it off because I didn't want to risk getting further involved with a cheater. Many nights after that I cried myself to sleep, but I continued to hold out hope for the one possible man in my future who would delight in my affection and value intimacy based on something other than sex.

It's tough to be a teenager, oblivious to what romantic love really means. Puppy love barely touches it. Maturity means learning that the desire for intimacy is much more than sexual desire, much more than strong chemistry. Love involves longing to know someone heart-to-heart. It's part of the overarching motivation to live and think and be alive in the world. It's a longing to know someone more fully than merely scratching the surface of their public persona.

Desire for affection is part of the reason we hunger for relationships. We long for the knowledge that we're accepted and loved for who we are, and that's no surprise because we're human *beings*, not human *doings*. We need human touch. Yet we can become so accustomed to pressing forward with life's daily responsibilities that we're apt to neglect, even forget, the incomparable value found in sharing our life with others. The many demands on our time pull us away from paying attention to this most basic fact of life. Without it, relationships can easily become unsatisfying.

In this chapter, I discuss the connection between affection and healthy relationships along with some of the ways we can communicate our love through affectionate touch. I also explore the importance of sexual intimacy in marriage and discuss reasons sexual activity doesn't guarantee intimacy. Whether in friendship, family, or marriage, affection can be expressed in numerous ways, and to that topic we now turn.

Desiring Affection

The longing to be close isn't confined to romantic relationships. A desire to be seen and known is part of the creative impulse that comes to each of us as a result of being created in God's image. Everyone has the need for deep recognition and affection. We all long to feel close to others. Such deep feelings of affection often creep up on us despite all efforts to be cool and calm. Christian author and apologist C. S. Lewis reminds us of the need for affection when he observed that "affection is responsible for nine-tenths of whatever solid and durable happiness there is in our lives."[2] Simply put, we need affection. It's not always easy to express how deeply we feel about those we love; physical affection gives us a place to express those feelings which aren't meant to be hidden deep within one's heart.

Moreover, affection doesn't mean quite the same thing for everyone. It's not always about inexplicable feelings, nor is it synonymous with sexual arousal. The word affection comes from the Latin *affectio*, an emotion that has the power to influence. But like so many other words, its meaning has morphed throughout the ages. Affection today includes both touch and other appropriate expressions of caring; it isn't just kisses and hugs. The way we share our affection greatly affects how another understands it and responds to it.

Sharing affection has numerous benefits, from health and well-being to self-esteem and the overarching quality of our primary relationships. Perhaps more than any other mode of friendship, affection signals that we're known in someone else's heart. Oddly, however, the need to give and receive affection is grossly misunderstood. Affection may still refer to that special feeling of tenderness and closeness one has for another, but the word is more often associated with outward displays of love, especially the affectionate demonstrations of someone "in love." While these benefits are immense, they are simultaneously underrated and overrated.

On the one hand, physical affection isn't everything in a relationship, but it sure is something. In some ways it's the glue that holds relationships together when tensions are high, particularly in marriage and family life. Physical affection was the start of the relationship with my football star. This kind of affection is a gentle touch on the shoulder, a softened facial expression, a hug, and leaning in instead of backing up.

All of this nonverbal communication has immense power to keep relationships strong. Most of us crave an affectionate, healthy touch. Affectionate touch is an aspect of relationships that unless triggered by sensory overload or an upbringing that has taught people it's wrong, most of us crave. It's even a natural de-stressor.[3] Scientists have long recognized nerve receptors in the skin that are stimulated by another's touch. When we're touched, oxytocin is released. Often called the "bonding hormone" or the "love chemical," oxytocin functions as a neurotransmitter sending a message to the brain.[4] We need this love chemical, just like an infant needs it from its mother.

The Importance of Everyday Affection

Along with thriving physically, the relational benefits that come from attending to the non-sexual need for affection is immense. Adding affection to daily life is akin to watering our plants daily and putting them in direct sunlight. Growing in the habit of affection reminds us that not everything in our work-a-day world is about being productive and efficient. Affection is a visceral, tangible reminder that tender care and love are the cornerstone of relationships. This is just as true in friendship as it is in families and married life.

There are many ways to show affection. Bringing a friend a meal or a cup of tea after a stressful day, greeting your daughter with a loving look and smile, making eye contact with your dad—all of these demonstrate affection. Perhaps a quick note or phone call to say "hello" or "I was thinking of you" is in order. It's important to show affection to the ones we love. Thankfully, there are numerous ways to do this both verbally and nonverbally.

This realization of the need to show affection should come as no surprise. Physical touch is important for everyone. When the Apostle Paul wrote to the young believers in Corinth about how they ought to treat one another, he encouraged the "holy kiss" (2 Cor. 13:12, NIV). This was neither a sensual act nor a precursor to romance. The holy kiss was an act of brotherly or sisterly affection. Whether we're single and hoping for a serious romantic relationship or living with a vow of celibacy for other reasons, we still need the warm verbal and gentle touch of others.

Corrie ten Boom, the Dutch Christian who was imprisoned in German death camps for leading the effort to smuggle her Jewish neighbors into freedom, was ultimately freed from the camp and lived to talk about her horrifying experience at the hands of the Nazis. During the inhuman treatment that she and her sister received, Corrie recounted that one of the things that helped her survive was remembering the way her father touched her face and prayed over her each night when she was a child. She clung to the memory of that nightly, tender touch.[5]

It has become easy to neglect the need for affirmation and the comfort of physical presence. We're living in a time when so much of the material world competes for our time and attention. We wrongly assume that once our relationships are established, they can just take care of themselves. Or that the virtual life is just as good as being with others. We can contact friends via email, send quick, witty messages via text, and even enjoy receiving photos of events happening across the world in seconds.

But, after a while the substitution of screen life for a life that's embodied begins to fray even the most closely-knit relationships. Writing and reading words via email and texting may include loving messages, but without the benefit of human interaction they eventually fall flat. It's a bit like those inflatable yard decorations at Christmas. Once the new day dawns, Charlie Brown and Lucy or Santa and his reindeer lay flat and deflated in the front yard. Our feelings in relationships need more than a fleeting text to sustain us when loneliness seeps into our consciousnesses. We're not cartoon characters or blow-up balloons.

God's Plan for Sex

We humans are created as spiritual beings with emotions, desires, deep thoughts, and souls all housed in our bodies. We're physical beings, made in the image and likeness of God, the *imago Dei*. After creating us, He looked humankind up and down and said, "This is good!" Indeed, we're His created people, made to dwell in the mystery and marvel of creation.

Part of this creative mystery is revealed in the inexplicable beauty of the sexual act. When two people join their lives and become one, another dimension is added to the loving, affectionate, life-giving glory of human relationships. Sexual intercourse is a beautiful, natural way to start a family, but it's much more. It's even more than two bodies connecting in orgasmic release.

Sex is holy. Sexual expression is holy and good. The word holy means "set apart," and indeed it is. Sex is set apart for something beyond the mundane. The media have distorted sexual love and gravely misinterpreted it to be synonymous with freedom and pleasure, cheapening lovemaking into something mundane instead of sacred. Sexual union is set apart for the deepest affection we have for others. As the Apostle Paul says in his letter to the young Roman Christians, "the marriage bed is undefiled" (Heb. 13:4, KJV). This partly means that sexual activity is natural for married couples. Anyone can have sex, but without the sacredness of the marriage bed, sex is much less than God in His graciousness and mercy intended. It also means that sexual union isn't to be minimized in marriage. It's not incidental, humdrum, or only to be engaged in when it's time to reproduce another human being.

Celebrating Our Bodies

Our bodies aren't to be overlooked or idolized. A problem arises when we put either too much or too little attention on physical pleasures. When it comes to sexual morals, Western culture seems to have cast off all restraints. In fact, that might be why so much sexual dysfunction is being treated medically and therapeutically. It's grievous to think how much this precious gift from our Maker has been drenched in dirt and paraded around as an act of personal power or commoditized for the sake of money and entertainment. Yet, it's almost as sad to hear about those who carry heavy psychological and religious baggage that keep them from experiencing the God-ordained joy of sexual union that's a blessing for those within the covenant of marriage.

I place emphasis on human physicality because God does. Scripture is clear that you and I are the work of a Master; our bodies are His handiwork. Our bodies are finite, but they are to be cherished, appreciated, and treated with respect, even awe. Is this a little bit overboard? I don't think so. Although Christianity historically has on occasion debased the body, viewing even married bodily pleasure in dark, unseemly ways, the human body is an amazing, resilient, and complex organism, full of dichotomies, tensions, reflexes, needs, capabilities, and desires, all designed by our Creator.

Trends in today's high-tech world tend to demean the beauty of our humanness, finding ways to increase efficiency in all that we do, even sex. Sexual adventures into the world of virtual reality are hyped as less complicated than the "messy meat world" where one must really deal with the imperfections and weaknesses of a real live person.[6] If we hope to experience the fruitfulness and fullness of a love that lasts, we must take it out of the abstract, virtual sphere and bring it into the realm of everyday life. It's perhaps easiest to perceive in the covenantal bond between husband and wife.

Thriving Sexually in Marriage

Physical touch for many has brought pleasure and relational intimacy. For others, it has brought an unwelcome and abusive touch that left an indelible mark. Even the mention of sex can be a trigger for those who have been abused. Working through that challenge for one or both married partners requires much healing and patience. Barring the pain of past infractions, it's important not to ignore the importance of giving and receiving to one another in our brokenness. Inside the marriage relationship, however, the affection and love associated with sexual union is to be cherished, even celebrated.

One of the worse comic sketches I ever heard involved a joke about marriage. In a mocking, stereotypical tone, the comedian joked about what it's like to be middle-aged and married. Apparently, he couldn't imagine a relationship where overcoming conflicts leads to great sex. He said something like, "You know it, men; marriage is all argument and no sex."

The ups and downs of an active life of physical intimacy don't have to vanish after five years, even 30. Surely each couple's needs and desires are different. Each couple must decide what works for them. Sex is negotiated as a wonderful display of growing and changing together. A young couple may start out their marriage with nightly or weekly sexual activity and become less frequent over time, but communication about the change is essential. Conversations about changing desires aren't easy, but necessary for maintaining closeness. Hormones aren't raging at age 50 like they were at 25, but that doesn't mean the sexual union among middle-aged couples should be any less exciting or fulfilling. In fact, after years of practice, marital sex can just get better.

Emotional Intimacy

While sexual intimacy is an important component of marital closeness, one doesn't always imply the other. Most emotional intimacy isn't connected to the sex act.[7] The ongoing need to give and receive affection—the gentle touch, the loving look, the tender tone of voice—are each part of how affection might be demonstrated and how intimacy thereby grows. But what if you don't come from a physically demonstrative family or what if non-sexual physical affection was not part of your upbringing? Even if we've been raised to live without hugs and tender touch, we can learn to be more affectionate and reap the relational benefits of its power.

The physical need for touch has been proven through many studies, particularly regarding infants who have been deprived of human touch. Nursing professor Lynda Harrison discovered the effect of a lack of touch on babies who are born prematurely: "many of the babies who were put into orphanages in Europe after World War II developed what we call 'failure to thrive.' They received calories, but they were not nourished with parental touch. They did not grow, and many developed severe social problems."[8]

For babies, the benefit of physical contact can be a matter of life and death, but the need for physical contact is important for all ages, especially as applied to the quest for deeper, more significant relationships. Our bodies can survive on beans and rice for months, but there are detrimental effects to going without a well-balanced diet. The same is true for our psychological well-being. Our bodies are capable of functioning without affection, but it starves our souls. We may be able to survive a terrible breakup or get along well enough to stay married, but love that flourishes is part of a pattern and promise of life itself. This is suggested in John's letter to Timothy, where he greets Gaius, "Beloved I hope you are prospering in every respect and are in good health, just as your soul is prospering" (3 John 1:2, NAB).[9] The flourishing and prosperity of our souls is part of the plan and purpose of all creation. We need both physical and emotional affection to flourish in life.

Incarnate Affection

Our bodies are much more than mere containers that house our souls. Despite our inherent frailties and the obvious limitations of our physicality, our bodies aren't to be despised, forsaken, or downgraded to something less. We have been fearfully and wonderfully made!

Consider for a moment the incarnation of Christ. Here, the great Holy Spirit and Creator of the Universe deemed physical presence important enough to send His Son to live in the very midst of the human race. The Word is alive and active, speaking to us today. The incarnation of Christ gives great weight to the importance of physical presence—for God lived, breathed, and walked on earth, situated in time and space. It was here that Jesus was crucified, died, buried, and here that He rose again. It was to human flesh that the Lord revealed Himself, inviting humans to once again live in unbroken fellowship with their Creator. God could have sent His magnificent message in a bottle. Instead, He sent His beloved Son. This gives us insight into God's heart. Author and spiritual director Ruth Haley Barton describes it this way:

All the great themes of Scripture affirm the significance of the body as a place where the presence of God can be known and experienced. The incarnation itself—Christ's choice to take on flesh and inhabit a human body—forever elevates the experience of embodiment to the heights of spiritual significance.[10]

Beyond the immeasurable worth of redemption is the relational significance of the incarnation for our own understanding of our God-created humanness. The embodiment of God's Word in Christ teaches that love must be practiced and lived out in relationships. It doesn't blossom in isolation. Relationships are established and love has the chance to grow. Relationships expand amid all the suffering, pain, and joy of physical presence. The body is sacred and love is situated firmly in the body. Love is more than a feeling. Love is more than an abstraction. Many of us may believe in the extraordinary power of love, but have a hard time putting our words into action. Love is much more than saying the correct words or the ability to express love eloquently.

The Sexiness of Everyday Life

In his insightful book *The Holy Longing: The Search for a Christian Spirituality*, priest and author Ronald Rolheiser notes that "Sexuality is an all-encompassing energy inside us . . . identified with the principle of life itself."[11] For a Christian, he says that "sex is sacred," is linked to monogamy, can lead to sanctity, and needs a healthy chastity ("The appropriateness of any experience") to express itself fully.[12] This energy, this principle of life is embodied in the daily interactions between marital partners as they serve each other. The little acts of kindness, resolution of an argument, making dinner, doing the laundry, letting your partner hold the remote—are all expressions of sexuality within a marriage. To my delight, my husband sets up the coffee maker so that fresh coffee greets me each morning, and he reads to me each night before bed (60 books in 45 years together).

Within this framework of promise to always be there, the marriage bed is a place of delight, laughter, and deep intimacy—supported by the sexiness of everyday life. To foster greater trust and intimacy, explore these questions.

1. What can you do today to make your partner feel special and loved?

2. Do you feel free and open to discuss anything, including your sex life?

3. What can you do to surprise your partner?

4. Where is Christ in your marriage?

— **Elizabeth McLaughlin**, Professor of Communication, Bethel University

Consider, as well, the intricate design of everything in the world, from the exquisite union and delight of sexual intimacy between a husband and wife to the mystery and grandeur of childbirth. These wonders reflect the inexplicable mystery of God's love. For humans, such mysterious love is expressed in the bodily coming together of two human beings who have taken the time to really know each other and flourish further by translating emotional, intellectual and psychological knowledge into physical knowledge. This experience is a celebration of life. It's "not one in which two people seek to love each other in spirit and truth in spite of the frailties or weakness of their bodies but, on the contrary, one in which all resources of body, mind, heart, imagination, emotion, and will are engaged in order to celebrate the love that has been given them by God, and in so doing to praise Him."[13] Even as this picture of married love somewhat eludes us, the posture—the leaning into God's lovely design—is a sign of hopeful bravery as well as love-drenched motivation.

Cloaked Needs for Affection

So many relational issues can be successfully addressed by attending to our needs for emotional and physical affection. If your friend, child, or spouse seems to need an unending supply of compliments or recognition, the problem may be unfulfilled affection. Often, we strive for recognition, sending out messages that scream, "See me," "Notice me," "Pay attention to *me*!" Yet what we might just need is simple affirmation. An affirming word, nod, or gentle touch can bring healing and satisfaction because it addresses who we are as opposed to what we do or what we may accomplish.

Our God-given physicality points to a recurring, essential theme in this book: with-ness. Being in relationships with others adds essential value to everyday existence, especially when we're with one another. With-ness is too significant to not spend enough time on. It's too basic to overlook. While we're most certainly spiritual beings with emotions, desires, deep thoughts, and an eternal destination, we're persons made to function within mystery and to marvel at the physical creation. We're designed to have embodied experiences with each other.

Sending messages to each other may help us keep in closer contact with friends and family, but when we assume it's adequate with-ness for maintaining healthy relationships, we'll find disappointment and heartache. Without physical embodiment, relationships begin to flatten. Many who have experienced a breakup are bewildered about how such deep love could be ruined, but increasingly it's clear that with lack of physical togetherness communication breakdowns begin. Knowing that your friend or spouse is with you is a salve and balm for which there is no substitute. So much of the dysfunction and confusion in our friend-ships and marriages can emerge simply because of the natural need to be affirmed with touch as well as words. Communicating love and affection is deeply nonverbal.

Conclusion

Being made in God's image privileges us with certain advantages and re-sponsibilities, including our capacity for loving relationships. In this chap-ter, I looked at the importance of physical affection, the difference between sexual intimacy and emotional intimacy, and the way that routine affection can help create greater stability and security in relationships. I also explored the connection between sexual union and affection. In the next chapter, I look closer at personal identity and healthy self-esteem.

Questions for Reflection

1. How may attending to your loved one's need for affection strengthen the relationship?

2. Why is the act of sexual oneness in marriage something that God sanctions and says "is good?" On what do you base your answer?

3. Consider your beliefs and opinions about sex. What messages have had the biggest influence on how you think about it?

Chapter 7

Thinking About Who You Are

Therefore, if anyone is in Christ, he is a new creation. The old has passed away; behold, the new has come.

— 2 Corinthians 5:17, ESV

HIGH SCHOOL was a rough time for many young people, and I was no exception. Fear of my father was perhaps the biggest factor in keeping me from experimenting with drugs, but my own conscience kept me from those temptations as well. I didn't want to risk a future of addiction or ruin, and figured if I never started, I wouldn't have to worry about getting hooked. At 14 and 15, I reflected on such things; I couldn't understand why so many of my peers didn't seem to think about their future. Despite having lots of good friends, I still felt lonely. My closest friends also chose not to participate in the drug culture or center their lives around getting drunk, but I knew I wasn't one of the "cool kids." Even though it was my personal choice, it felt odd not being part of the crowd.

Back then, I didn't know myself very well yet, but I already knew that I loved to be with people and I tried to make that happen every chance I got. Growing up as a first-born child with a very strict father, the only freedom I was allowed was my bicycle. I put many miles on that purple 10-speed. If there wasn't play practice or a school newspaper meeting, I was on my bike watching a baseball game with fellow students or finding friends far across town who just wanted to hang out. Understanding my own identity was still quite muddy but I simply loved being with others.

You would think that knowing yourself would be the most natural thing in the world. But in this age of bots, digital avatars, and other virtual representations, knowing our real self isn't easy. We tend to believe that the self is a thing of our own making, constructed by layers of family traits, personality traits, coping mechanisms, fashion, style, and societal expectations. Many of us use resources to construct our identity and listen to what others say about who we are. It's not that these layers are nonexistent or insignificant; rather, they are merely part of the tapestry that covers what Trappist monk Thomas Merton and others refer to as the "true self."[1] Understanding the self as the living soul at the core of our being is much deeper than the ways we present ourselves to the world. This "living soul" is the true self. Tapping into both the inner self and the external, presentational self helps us regulate our emotions, manage our personalities, and address our childhood wounds.

In this chapter, I look at the difference between self-focus and being self-centered. Next, I plunge into the matter of identity to discover how self-perceptions and ultimately self-realization greatly influences our social and familial relationships. Finally, I explore what it means to build a house of relationship while learning to let God show us the way.

Self-focus

Understanding that we're created by a loving Creator who says we're "fearfully and wonderfully made" helps us find footing in the world and puts us on a path toward understanding who we are as individuals (Ps. 139:14, NIV). Taking time to understand who we are isn't the same as being self-centered or selfish. Instead, self-work is a worthy path toward healthy self-esteem which we need to maintain strong, satisfying relationships.

We need to strike a balance between focusing on ourselves and not focusing on others. To put it differently, we should aim to love both ourselves and others. We can't love ourselves if we don't know our true inner selves. We can't love others if we don't know them. And we have to be careful not to define ourselves purely in terms of what others want us to be. Fortunately, I avoided the drug-and-party scene by maintaining my own, distinct identity. Part of it was knowing I would have to answer to my father. That helped. It kept me at arm's length from a circle of popularity, but it saved me from potential harm.

There must be sufficient time for reckoning with who we are, but taking time to focus on ourselves and our identity doesn't mean we saturate ourselves with endless hours of self-help literature or various attempts to reinvent ourselves. Contemporary Western society has emphasized "the false self" ad nauseam. It seems, in fact, a foundational principle "of modern culture is the expressing and remaking of 'the self' in order to achieve self-realization and self-fulfillment."[2] This doesn't mean we ignore self-reflection or the importance of self-discovery. It also doesn't mean we turn ourselves into a project and try to squeeze into a tight little box of compliance.

Self-work means we're acutely aware of the need to grow, stretch, and learn, along with our willingness to do it. It means we take time to attend to the beautiful body, heart, and mind God gave us, and commit ourselves not to abuse it. Self-work that makes a positive difference in our relationships doesn't mean pampering, prodding, or punishing ourselves. It means becoming aware, getting ready, and then walking in a willingness to actively address areas needing attention. Self-work is important work in its own right, and it can reap deep relational benefits, including building beautiful, fruitful relationships with a friend or spouse.

Whose We Are

Understanding who we are doesn't magically happen at age 12 or 25, but is a slow, steady process over a lifetime of self-awareness occurring through our interactions with God and those we trust. The tough part is taking off the masks that hide us, even the ones that hide us from ourselves. Like a young fawn peeking out from behind a tree, the naked self is shy, even if the personality is big. In my experience, understanding *who* we are involves a process that's uniquely and fully linked to *whose* we are.

Personality is an outgrowth of who we are. It emerges from the many ways we learn to function and behave as we develop.[3] As we make ourselves known to others, our traits and self-concept, values, and emotions—all part of our personality—can help us grasp a bit of insight into how to change our reactions or improve our behavior. But our personality doesn't completely define us. Similarly, working as a plumber, kindergarten teacher, landscaper, tennis coach, doctor, or drugstore clerk doesn't thoroughly define us. They are roles by which we're known in the world.

Our identity in Christ is unfailing. Roles will change. Friends will change. Social status may change, but our identity becomes solid as we find ourselves in Him. Once we realize that God has created us in His Image, we realize that we're known and loved by Him. Unlike our purely social roles and masks, this "in Christ" identity is not easily rocked. A failed driver's test, being passed over for the promotion, or having little money in our bank account don't have the power to claim our well-being, steal our peace, or usurp who we are. Instead, we learn to see ourselves as God sees us—as his beloved children.[4]

When our identity is securely situated in Christ, social media "likes" and images have far less sway over our moods. An increasing confidence and stability emerge as we begin to walk in greater fullness of whose we are. As we walk, we discover a path to greater freedom, anticipating the future with a sense of adventure and excitement, knowing that He is there, and that He will never leave. Defining ourselves in relationship to the One True God helps us rest in the assurance that a crummy job, bad habit, or failed test doesn't define us. If I had experimented with drugs in high school, I would still be God's child. These human frailties don't make us any less His daughter or son. The dynamics of our identities have all to do with God, and He changes not.[5]

Cultural change or personal change can be upending, but they don't have to rule us if we cling to our identity in Christ. When we know that God is our Father and that we're part of His beloved family, we begin to understand the breadth, depth, and full measure of His eternal love for us. We're changed; we're transformed. Such a God-anchored identity may not happen overnight or even in a year. Instead, it's a process of growing in community with the Lord and His people. We become secure in the knowledge of our Beloved. Moreover, walking in our true identity prepares us to love others in ways that are fruitful, healing, and situated in a sense of fullness rather than scarcity. God fills us with more love to share with others. He prepares us not only to selflessly give love and care to others, but also to receive love from another. Although my father was strict, God taught me through him to identify limits so I wouldn't abuse my freedom.

The ability to give love is an obvious aspect of close relationships. But what often goes undetected as a roadblock to relationships is our inability to receive it from others. As much as we need to be loved, without a sound sense of self, we can hardly receive the love others have to give. There are many reasons for this. Such emotional blockage often points back to earlier hurt and trauma, emotional wounds that we have perhaps never identified or addressed. These blockages can become recurring conscious and subconscious messages that pile up and remain with us as false stories about what others think of us and who they say we are. Many of these stories are lies, or simply the ill-informed perspectives of others who don't really know our heart's inner workings.

Professional counselor and lecturer Robert McGee points to the ways we all tend to sabotage our relationships through core lies and false beliefs. These untruths create a false foundation by associating our self-worth with our performance. They wreak havoc in our relationships because they lead us to act out of the four untruths of shame, blame, performance, and the approval of others.[6] We need the steady, timeless hand of God to steer our hearts in the right direction. Some Christian traditions call this spiritual formation; it happens as an outgrowth of our communion with God. Through Scripture, worship, fellowship, and prayer, to name several, He equips us to overcome such untruths and other lies.

Spiritual formation practices help draw us closer to God, and better hear the still small voice reminding us that we're "accepted in the Beloved" (Eph. 1:6b, NKJV). Whether we perform well at work or have a stellar Christian witness, we're loved and cherished by the God who made us. Our worth is found in our relationship to God, our Maker. He says we have purpose as part of His eternal family, not in the roles and the masks our culture demands. In our success-oriented society it's difficult to grasp this because so many advertising and marketing campaigns are designed to make us feel badly about ourselves, thus creating a vacuum, making us feel that something is missing. How bad? Bad enough to buy their product. Bad enough to build our esteem on their brand. Bad enough to keep on striving for more. Bad enough to hate ourselves.

In response, we anchor our significance in something other than work, busyness, or the number of social media "likes" received. Discovering that our significance, worth, peace, and well-being all come from God's definition of us as His children is a powerful antidote to the flimsy and changing identities cast in popular culture. The deep awareness of this fact doesn't come from blinking our eyes and saying, "it is so." It doesn't come from intellectual assent or wishing it were so. This truth is discovered in the depths of our spirit and emerges from a close communion with the One who made us.

Self-work

Some of us are better at articulating what we're feeling about who and whose we are while others are more reticent or confused. It's a challenge to begin self-work and not fall into either judgement or hyper-focus. Both postures may give us cause to refrain from starting the process altogether. But we must dive in if we want to lay a foundational identity. Without it we're apt to build on a faulty foundation, one that may not withstand life's storms. But we don't have to do this alone. The Holy Spirit faithfully guides us and teaches us as we open ourselves up to His work in us.[7] As we examine and reflect upon our growing self-knowledge, we'll find it spilling over into our social relationships. As our attitudes and behavior begin to conform to the biblical teaching of brotherly love and righteous relationships, we shouldn't be surprised to see kindness, authenticity, and humility emerge in our earthly relationships.[8]

Trying to understand who we are isn't self-centeredness. Nor is it surrendering to the individualism of our times. It also isn't a matter of giving into the laser-like focus on ourselves that's so common in our day. Philosopher Charles Taylor speaks to this hyper-individualism, suggesting that genuine self-discovery shouldn't just involve "[. . .] a centering on the self and a concomitant shutting out, even unawareness of the greater issues or concerns that transcend the self, be they religious, political, historical."[9] Instead, our path to the true self is discovered in the real life challenges we face and the opportunities before us. We offer our full lives to God in the context of where we find ourselves. To put it another way, our God-focused self-work isn't a form of world-ignoring, "spiritual" therapy. It is an all inclusive, comprehensive apprehension of all that God has done and is doing in our lives and in the world. It involves recognition of (and attention to) the inner life we each possess. This type of self-work is the opposite of selfishness. It is healthy. It is brave. It is something we participate in with God.

Identity: The House of Relationship?

Having a sturdy sense of who we are is important for all our relationships. This is because who we are forms the foundation of all our relationships. As followers of Christ, we understand He is the Rock of our salvation and the Shepherd of our souls. Certainly, the Lord, our Maker, is the true source of our being. As we grow in this knowledge and apply it in the real world, our understanding of our solid position in Christ becomes a habit of the heart and prepares us to move into greater intimacy with others.

Indeed, discovering it's "in Him we live and move and have our being" is a powerful antidote to the aimless rounds of searching for our identity in dead-end relationships (Acts 17:28, NIV). This knowledge provides foundational substance for existing and new relationships. I call this the "house of relationship." Cultivating a friendship or building a life together in marriage requires a foundation, in much the same way that building a house requires a foundation. While our relational foundation doesn't call for three feet of cement or metal pilings, it does require something strong enough to withstand the normal wear and tear of seasonal storms. A well-built house of relationship is strong enough to last. It's stable enough to withstand the many winds that blow through our lives each day.

The desire for a safe haven of total belonging is so strong and attractive that we're tempted to move quickly past the necessary steps of development. We have a hard time being patient. We might be so eager to rush in and decorate, plant flowers along the front path, all before laying a solid foundation. For instance, if cyclical heartache or the pain of a breakup from a serious relationship lingers, it may be even more tempting to slap up some paper-thin walls, a shabby roof and call it a home. Why look back when moving forward? Because the outer appearance of a home doesn't ensure the house will be able to stand through the years. That's not how it works. With each new friend or partner we have to start from scratch. Our external and internal neighborhood has changed. Without tending to the foundation, we find once again the house of relationship in shambles.

Pouring a foundation may be the most time-consuming, least glamourous, strenuous work in building relationships. Long before lumber and cinderblock are purchased and cement is mixed, it's necessary to excavate the site. That's right, dig. A solid foundation must be poured into a space that can hold it. So it is with our relationships. We must go below the surface and dig deeply within ourselves, excavating the ground upon which the house of relationship will be built. It sounds a little daunting but let's face it, it can be messy work. After all, who wants to get dirty and sweaty digging up a place and then pour gallons of cement in a hole and wait for it to dry!?

Personal resistance to this process is understandable. Our perceptions are packed with illusions. We wonder, "Doesn't love just happen?" "Don't solid friendships just find us?" "Love is something that happens to us, right?" "Can't we simply skip this step?" We can (and many do) skip these important steps, but not without consequences. Countless instances of domestic abuse, public humiliation, explosive breakups, and tears are spilled over lost love and find their way into therapists' offices every day. The drama is real, and it isn't uncommon. While this self-work will continue throughout our lives, sturdy, satisfying relationships need to begin on solid ground.

Ultimately, this type of building is a spiritual exercise. Jesus used a similar house metaphor when talking to the people about the wise and foolish builders. He was speaking in the context of obedience, and the solid rock foundation referred to God:

Therefore, everyone who hears these words of mine and puts them into practice is like a wise man who built his house on the rock. The rain came down, the streams rose, and the winds blew and beat against that house; yet it did not fall, because it had its foundation on the rock. But everyone who hears these words of mine and does not put them into practice is like a foolish man who built his house on sand. The rain came down, the streams rose, and the winds blew and beat against the house, and it fell with a great crash. (Matt. 7:24–26, NIV)

Digging Up Dirt on Ourselves

Taking this house metaphor further might make the idea of laying the foundation for our relationships even more formidable. As we're building the foundation in ourselves, we're likely to discover sand, clay, rocks, worms, and bugs. Maybe even some old bones. This interior digging is undoubtedly self-revealing and sometimes painful. In fact, excavation of our own heart, soul, and mind can be upending. First, we need the help of the ultimate excavator, the Lord Himself. We ask the Holy Spirit to show us what is there and ask for the courage to face it head on. Jesus promised this would help when he told his disciples: "When He, the Spirit of Truth comes, he will guide you into all truth" (John 16:13, NIV).

Along with this heavenly counsel, we likely need earthly help. A spiritual director and a good therapist can support the excavation efforts. Even a very wise and compassionate friend might be available to listen and help us sort out what we find in this dig below the surface of our personality.

During one of my early periods of excavation, I learned a hard lesson about myself. All through my teens and twenties I saw myself as non-judgmental. What I didn't realize is that even though I was able to keep a spirit of condemnation toward others at bay, my own inner dialogue happily heaped judgment upon myself. I'd often slip into degrading self-talk with phrases like, "You'll never reach that goal," or "They don't want to hear what you have to say." Knee-deep in foundation work, the Holy Spirit showed me that whether the judgement was pointed toward another or pointed toward myself, it was still the same deathly spirit of condemnation. I had been taking on a job that Jesus never gave me. "There is no condemnation for those that are in Christ Jesus" (Rom. 8:1, NIV).

Since this process can be quite upsetting, one may ask, is all this self-work necessary? As fallen people, we simply need to do it. We invariably carry our burdens and faults into our relationships and naturally draw our identity from the people with whom we're currently most attached. Psychologists call this tendency codependence. It's a relational dysfunction that's the result of over-reliance or excessive focus on another person.[10]

Codependence manifests itself in numerous ways, but primarily by over-focusing on one person or group. For example, during adolescence or young adulthood, if my friends say I am cool, kind, and generous, I gladly define myself by who they say I am. But when (if) they leave or stop demonstrating affection, I'm in trouble. The very foundation of who I believe I am begins to crumble. Addressing such codependence early in life puts us at an advantage on the road to self-realization, and ultimately, helps us to develop stronger relationships.

Defining ourselves by our work or job is no better. This, too, sets our self-worth on unstable ground. Jobs come and go these days. So do ministry opportunities. We need to be mission-minded, but not mission-centric. Most devastating of all, we might firmly believe that we know God's calling on our lives but later discover we're ill-suited for the work. Unrest creeps into our soul. The one calling we know for certain is following Jesus, even though we can't know for certain where he will lead us.

"My work is my life!" Who hasn't heard this before? When we define our work as our life and our identity, when we look to a job, position, or employer to meet all our needs for acceptance, encouragement, affection, and companionship, we take on burdens we were not meant to carry. When we confuse our identity with what we do for another in our jobs, we set ourselves up for problems in our relationships because we're functioning from a weak and rocky foundation.

Living from Identity, Not for Identity

My particular wounding lends itself to compulsively looking to others to ground my identity. I'm hoping people will reflect back to me—through a smile, a laugh, or a kind word— "Peter, you are lovable. You're important to me. I love being with you." It can be hard for me to believe this without a steady stream of positive input. Sometimes, it almost feels like I don't exist or have a sense of identity without kind, friendly people "shining their face upon me." I often tell myself, "If I am smart enough, kind enough, competent enough; if I give enough, help enough, bring enough people peace and joy, then people and God will keep their faces shining upon me." In these moments, I am living like a person without a center, driven along by a sense deprivation—looking hopefully at something external to myself to stabilize me. It's living for a sense of identity, rather than from identity.

Of course, I can't live off other people's glimmers. It's easy to live for a sense of identity, hoping that by doing certain things, we'll finally be someone. It's much harder to live from a place of identity—where we accept the grace that's unflinchingly extended to us by Christ, and thus, freeing us from ourselves and being able to turn our attention toward loving others. When I live grounded in the understanding that I am loved and lovable at my core, I settle into the reality that my life's journey can be more about uncovering "the Peter-est Peter" buried beneath the rubble of trauma and fear, and less about constantly, compulsively looking for reassurance that Love has not run out on me. But this all takes time.

— **Peter Copan**, Therapist, Renew Counseling,
Winter Park, Florida

Codependence is just one of the sticky identity issues that can ruin a friendship or marriage. Philosopher and author Charles Taylor offers one explanation for identity problems today. He suggests what has happened in our culture is that

old ties are broken down. At the same time, city dwellings are transformed by the immense concentrations of population of the modern metropolis. By its very nature this involves much more impersonal and casual contact, in place of the more intense, face-to-face relations in earlier times. All this can't help but generate a culture in which the outlook of social atomism becomes more real and more entrenched.[11]

Taylor's contribution to the conversation is helpful, but just one factor in the discussion of identity.

Living in an age of such great speed and efficiency doesn't make it easier to understand who we are, partially because we need close relationships with God and others to best understand ourselves. Digital culture creates a multitude of new opportunities to share slivered pieces of ourselves—enjoying great breadth in the number of people we're loosely connected to but missing out on the depth and joy of truly being known. Social media outlets such as X (formally Twitter), Meta, Instagram, Tinder, Snapchat and so many others are stages for us to perform on. Social media may indeed provide temporary satisfaction to the miseries that flatten and narrow an anchored sense of self, but they can't eliminate them. By providing ways to bypass self-reflection and by allowing those seeking close relationships to jump in and choose someone immediately, they offer false dreams of relational bliss.

We all wear masks of one sort or the other. When we're willing to remove them, we may find that a whole new world of relationships open up to us. These masks keep others from seeing who we really are. As we do the self-work on our identity that's necessary for a strong foundation, the potential for a close relationship grows. When that willingness is absent, we can be lonely and dissatisfied even in the most seemingly perfect friendship or marriage. Much of that dissatisfaction stems from not feeling understood or feeling alone in the relationship. That feeling of loneliness isn't something to be ignored. Recent studies point to the growing epidemic of loneliness.[12] The UCLA Loneliness Index finds record numbers of people reporting how desperately lonely they are.[13] Posting a 30-second reel on social media in hopes of being seen and known just doesn't satisfy. Yet, we flood the gates of social media with our time and attention believing it will stem our loneliness. It may be fun or entertaining, but it's insufficient to fill up our yearning to know and be known.

Part of the reason for this rush to mediated space is because we're looking for affirmation. It's all too easy to miss the need for God and others to establish a strong sense of self. Our identity comes from knowing who we are, but we need others who really know us to reflect and help us remember that we belong. As educator and activist Parker Palmer explains, "self is not a scrap of turf to be defended but a capacity to be enlarged through relationship."[14] Focusing first on building a strong foundation in Christ is a road that leads to strength, hope, grace, and life.

Conclusion

In this chapter, I talked about the importance of building our friendships, marriages, and other relationships on a foundation that's solid. This foundation begins with understanding who we are and whose we are. Remember that attending to self can help us unveil those outward quirks and personality flaws that keep us from flourishing at work, at home, or in our circle of friends.

In the next chapter I explore ways to dwell lovingly in the house of relationship, drawing from a healthy and proper realization of God's gift of communication. In the coming pages we look at ways to create a safe environment for intimacy to grow. For now, take some time to ponder the following questions and then take the next step to discuss them with someone you cherish.

Questions for Reflection

1. Write a paragraph to your spouse (future or current) sharing the deepest parts of who you think you are. Read it aloud and write another paragraph describing how you feel about sharing it.

2. When you think of your closest friend, how do you think he or she might describe you? Is the description in sync with how you describe yourself?

3. In imagining true emotional intimacy with your friend, parent, child, or spouse, what are some of the ways he or she would describe who you are and vice versa?

Chapter 8

Growing Closer Emotionally

Set me as a seal upon your heart, as a seal upon your arm, for love
is strong as death.

— Song of Solomon, 8:6a, ESV

THE ROOM flickers with the light of a single candle. When you walk through
the door, the glow in the house and the tantalizing aroma of your favorite
food greets you. The table is decorated with cloth napkins and fancy flat-
ware. A single rose graces the center of the table.

There he is, standing in the doorway with a slightly mischievous grin.
You give him a little kiss hello and ask, "Who is coming over?" With a
twinkle in his eyes, he draws you near and says, "It's all for you, my love.
Just for you."

By now you are either chuckling and shaking your head or tears are
filling your eyes. Wouldn't it be wonderful if coming home every night was
this way? If we could do that for each other, reduce the stress of the day, and
remind each other of how very good it is to be sharing life, wouldn't it add
more than a small packet of sweetness to life?

It may not occur daily, but a loving reception like the one above
doesn't have to stay in the fantasy section of the public library. Intimacy in
marriage is filled with passion and caring acts. This version of love is divine;
it's not a fairy tale. The only fairy tale is the one that tells us nothing can go
wrong. Contrary to popular depictions, romantic passion isn't synonymous
with the lusty fire of lovemaking. Hopefully, there is that sort of passion
in married love, but passion isn't foremost about sex. For many, however,
passion is just about sex.

Passion for life increases when there are people to share it with. A
close marital relationship is joyful; loving families provide deep security;
dear friends are the rare jewels of life. Whether it's marriage, a lively circle
of friends, or a loving family, our lives need to be shared and celebrated
passionately. Along with rationality, social connection is part of the mark
of being human.[1] We flourish and thrive with deep, fruitful relationships.

Passion will always play a part in unravelling the often-tangled threads of what keeps us close.

Intimacy: Life's Beautiful Treasure

More than anything else, a closely-knit, intimate relationship can satisfy the soul's yearning for belonging and fulfillment. We were made for it. Life-long friendships, romance that stays lively and strong, siblings who seem more like best friends—these are all among life's rewards. Although, they don't materialize just because we've made an initial pleasant connection. Relational closeness, or intimacy, isn't a great mystery, but it can be elusive. It has its own mystique, and it doesn't come easily. To develop and sustain a relationship that feels safe, warm, and close requires more than desire. Close relationships require commitment.

Control and Trust: The Golden Threads

Part of the golden threads that make intimacy so satisfying is the freedom that allows us to give and receive love. This freedom stems from letting go of the need to be in total control. It's a common desire to control what, when, and where life happens. Though life is filled with uncertainty and powerlessness, some of us try harder to control it than others. If you've been accused of being a controlling person (even affectionately dubbed a "control freak"), it may be time to loosen up and let go. This is challenging if you're the designated friend, partner, or family member who always oversees the details of every event. You may not enjoy making reservations, researching a trip, or sending the invitations to a party, but it won't get done if you don't do it. Letting go or loosening our grip on control doesn't mean we should stop regulating our emotions. Nor does it mean we ought to throw up our hands or pretend not to care. What it does mean is that we recognize and begin to work through the tight grip that control has on us.

It may be even worse if there's someone you love who is controlling. Perhaps you feel like a caged bird and don't enjoy waiting on the perch until your friend says, "now you can fly."

For many of us, giving up control is difficult. We prefer a black-and-white world of certainty, which also means we may miss the serendipitous, adventuresome experiences that can make life rich. Our friends and family relationships that mutually share decision making can add so much to our lives. Releasing control has other benefits, as well. Our friendships and family lives can more easily take on a climate of mutuality—a way of being with one another that respects each person's desires and preferences.

Giving up control is humility in action. Once we learn to loosen the grip of control, we can make strides in growing trust, another important part of intimacy. Humility is possible when we trust God more than we trust ourselves. It means we're looking to His power rather than our own feeble attempts to manufacture our future. As the Apostle Paul says, "Love is not jealous or rude. It does not insist on its own way" (1 Cor. 13:4–8a, RSV).

Trust follows humility as we seek intimacy. Trusting God, we learn to let go and grow. When we miss a planned outing because we slept through the morning, our disappointed friend might say, "no problem," but the unspoken, message is "you aren't reliable," or "you can't be trusted to do what you say you'll do." Trust isn't a commodity to be taken off the shelf. It takes time to build, and it's fragile. It's not something we can buy, but something that grows. Being "someone you can count on" is evidenced by a constancy that doesn't waver. How do we know when to trust others? Time will tell. Trusting another isn't automatic. It emerges between two people as a result of time spent together. Being there for one another, keeping a secret, holding true to your words—these are the ways trust is measured and nurtured. And such trust builds intimacy, and intimacy is where passion grows.

Passion

Recently, my husband and I were treated to a Broadway show, staged at a smaller theatre in another state. The songs were upbeat. The dancing and choreography were remarkable and the actors overflowed with passion for their craft. It wasn't a sad story, but several times I felt my eyes welling with tears. It was thoroughly delightful, helping us remember the goodness of God's creativity and gifts. On the ride home, we discussed how many hours the orchestra and actors must have rehearsed. They sacrificed time, energy, and probably sleep to bring us such enjoyment. Passion requires work and even possible suffering. One day, the people we most love might die before us. Passion can't escape suffering. Passion in Latin is *pati*, which means suffering.[2]

The Greek root of passion is *pathos*, which infers deeply felt emotion along with suffering. Words such as "sympathy," "empathy," and "pathetic" all have the same root, and each of them involves shared feeling. The feelings involved in *pathos* involve not only good and pleasurable emotions, but also fervent, intense, and sometimes agonizing ones. Passion is often grossly misunderstood. It isn't something we do, but more of a driving force within, a spark that motivates us into movement or action. Passion makes its appearance in relationships in numerous ways. When we share our life, giving 100% to our partner, our family, or our community, passion rises. Passion involves desire, zeal, and excitement, but also suffering. A clear example of this is the passion of Christ expressed on the cross. God's great passion for us was in an act of loving sacrifice that involved intense suffering and ultimately death. Like Jesus, our love for others will call us to surrender and sacrifice.

Neurobiologist Curt Thompson considers suffering a defining reality of life that's intimately linked to love and community. He writes that the ability to trust and grow in relationships with others begins in childhood with secure attachment provided by people who give us the 4 S's—being "seen, soothed, safe and secure."[3] But no one gets through childhood without having suffered some indignities and oversight by mostly well-meaning parents who loved us passionately.

We all desire more than sexual passion. Maybe this is because so many would-be relationships come up short of meeting our expectations. There seems to be a frenzy in our culture to try people out sexually instead of taking time to really know one another and going through the normal and much needed steps of relational growth. Thomas Merton suggests that the oversexualization of passion led to a dark and dreadful atomization of love:

> [It] puts the human body on the market, either as a desirable package of commodities and pleasures or as a highly dangerous compound of moral evil. Love becomes no longer an expression of the communion between persons but a smorgasbord of the senses in which one selects what he wants—or what he thinks he can get away with.[4]

Every day, men and women substitute momentary physical passion for the greater good of their relationship and reduce their relationship to a facsimile of love. Instead of feeling fulfilled, enriched, or loved, they go away lonely, broken, hurt, emotionally deformed and physically broken. We really want a love that's true and lasting, not a momentary fling. Kory Floyd, Arizona State University communication professor and researcher, consistently found that the "more affectionate people were, the happier, more socially active, less stressed, less depressed, and more satisfied with their romantic relationships they were."[5] The stability and affection in such relationships lead to greater happiness and overall well-being.

Unfortunately, passion isn't always shared. A mother can passionately give her heart and soul to an adult daughter who doesn't reciprocate. A man may feel deep passion for his wife, only to find a tepid reception. A woman can give 100% of her heart to her husband only to discover he has been unfaithful, giving his heart and body to another. Mother Theresa is an unusual example of non-mutual passion. Caring for the sick and dying in Calcutta, she tended to those who couldn't give anything in return. But God's passion blessed her and gripped her to continue giving despite her battle with doubt and depression.

The Sacred Circle

I have not detailed the joys of sexual passion. After all, each married couple dwells within a sacred, but private circle. The sacred circle is intimate. Each couple finds their own way to express the intense, passionate desire for one another. In a thriving marriage, passion's flame grows as love is mutually expressed with respect and dedication. Risking vulnerability, partners feel safe to release emotion without holding back.

Lovemaking in marriage is one of God's most glorious gifts. He could have made human reproduction something that was difficult or even dangerous. Instead, He designed marital love to be something beautiful, something we'd long for as a very natural part of our personhood. Marital passion involves the act of complete surrender—a giving up, a giving in, a total meshing of one's entire body and soul with another. At this level, deep, long-term intimacy often reveals itself in the surrender of our own comforts and personal desires for the sake of the other. But even in this holy marital context there are times when the sacred circle's passion may lag or disappear. This is why the healthiest place for our ultimate passions must be rooted in something stronger than sexual pleasure.

Therefore, the journey toward sexual intimacy begins long before a trip to the bedroom. It begins with respect, interest, kindness, curiosity, gentleness, self-control, and care. As such love emerges, the journey moves to strength, integrity, goodness, play, and joy. Without this preparation, sexual passion is reduced to much less than it's meant to be. When the foundation of a relationship and the golden threads that make it strong aren't present, the sexual act won't satisfy for long. The most satisfying marital intimacy comes from deep, emotional attachment, which requires mutual honesty and vulnerability.

Vulnerability is a bit easier for some, particularly those who grew up in a healthy family with a home life. But all adults who desire true intimacy must be vulnerable enough to risk being hurt. Practicing this sort of honest, open, vulnerable communication isn't easy, but it's a key part of the mix that makes sexual intimacy a reality.

Cultivating close relationships inside and outside of marriage also involves openness. Openness isn't quite a skill, but more a state of the heart. It's a bit like leaving the door to your house unlocked when you are expecting guests for dinner or putting out a welcome mat or wreath on the door. When your friends arrive, everything says: "Glad you're here! Come on in." On the other hand, if you're sitting with a friend over a cup of coffee and you turn on the television or look at your favorite magazine while she is talking, you're not only signaling disinterest, but also communicating a message that's quite the opposite of openness. You may personally be open but you won't likely find much success in your conversation. Healthy openness must be cultivated.

Creating a non-rushed atmosphere that shows interest and curiosity is the key to openness. Body language, eye contact, a ready smile—all these nonverbal cues help communicate to others that you're attentive and perhaps ready to share life more deeply. When we're open—leaning in, eyes connecting with eyes, following another's words with true attention and listening with empathy—we suggest openness. It isn't red roses, fancy jewelry, a special card on one's birthday, or romantic getaways that build intimacy. It's the willingness to be open and take risks to truly love others that is going to pave the road to long and lasting marriages, friendships that flourish, and family harmony.

Love that shapes and molds us is much more than a mere feeling or state of mind. It's heart-driven, self-sacrificial reality that changes everything. We must be willing to change if we want to know such love, or to experience its inexplicable richness. This is due to the nature of love itself. Love is a powerful force that doesn't adjust to our own convenience and particular comfort zones. It's something that happens between two people; it's transformative, not transactional.[6] In fact, this may be the number one reason so many relationships fail.

Part of the reason for this is our human resistance to change—it's strong. We might see change as a compromise or set personal comfort as a higher priority. But we have been changing since the day we were born.

On the physical level, our brains are constantly experiencing change. Skin cells are regenerating and replacing old ones daily. On the social level, our relationships grow or decline. Change is often an uncomfortable part of life. This is important to reckon with, for unwillingness to change is a major part of the reason relationships don't thrive or grow into their potential. But there is more than resistance to change that impedes our desire to be emotionally intimate with others. We're creatures of habit.

Particularly in romantic relationships, the last several decades have seen a large portion of Americans treat casual sexual encounters as an accepted norm. Even though some studies show a soft decline in casual sex among teenagers, there is still an entrenched and unsatisfying fascination with weekend hookups.[7] These casual sexual encounters interfere with the development of emotional intimacy for many reasons, but one is simply that it takes time to truly know one another. Moving too quickly to sexual involvement can sideline the desire for emotional closeness. Jumping to physical intimacy before the relationship has had time to develop is like slapping up the drywall in your house before there is any foundation or flooring. Intimacy takes time.

Another impediment to developing emotional closeness is that some people avoid intimacy altogether because of past rejection or heartbreak. We can also repress the need for relational closeness by convincing ourselves that it's unattainable or not worth the potential pain of breaking up. Even early childhood social development influences our desire and ability to become intimate. Researchers like John Bowlby demonstrate a strong link between absence of parental attachment in early childhood and the avoidance of intimacy in adulthood.[8] Shutting down our desire for close relationships seemingly protects us from hurt, but it can lead to misery and depression. Indeed, we were created by Love and for Love's sake. No matter how we try to protect ourselves from the risks of opening our lives to others, the drumbeat of love is there in the background, beckoning us, stirring up desire, pounding in our chest, coursing through our blood. In fact, denial of the need for intimacy may play a key part in the reason so many numb themselves emotionally with a party lifestyle. Without the richness of relational intimacy, we might throw ourselves into overdrive, seeking activities and substances that cloak the pain and dull our deep feelings of emptiness.

You might be hesitant, shy, or uncomfortable sharing too much about yourself, wary about how it might be received. Yet, taking the risk toward greater openness makes it possible to grow in closeness. As you practice being open, the light of your inner love begins to get brighter, and the seeds of love begin to blossom and grow. Like a green leaf stretching toward the sun's warmth, openness gives passion the space to rise. Strong desire and deep, abiding love can begin to emerge as a result of stretching beyond your self-doubts. Passion and openness go hand-in-hand.

The opposite of openness in our relationships is being closed. This isn't the same as being closed-minded or narrow in our ability to stretch our thinking. Maybe you've been in a relationship that was shrouded in secrets, or perhaps you may have even been accused of lacking openness. This may be particularly frustrating if you're a person of truth who values honesty. Yet, you can be honest and lack openness at the same time. For example, your college roommate is back from summer break and you catch up with a conversation about what you each did over the summer. You lost your internship after performing poorly the first two weeks, gained ten pounds, and struggled with depression, but you respond to her question with a weak smile saying, "It was great, thanks. How about yours?" Openness involves more than truth-telling. It's about letting another into your more private thoughts, making room for trusted others to hear and weigh in on what you've shared.

There are degrees of openness, all of which require various levels of vulnerability. I'm not speaking about complete transparency. To be totally transparent requires the greatest level of risk, and it's reserved for the very closest of relationships, during the most tender of times. Also, total transparency isn't the same as openness; it isn't necessary that every nuance of feeling or opinion is shared in order to achieve relational openness. In marriage, the deeper dimensions of love may be experienced as openness grows. Like the beauty of a rosebud opening into full flower, the oneness in marriage has the potential with openness to become more fragrant and lovely with every decade, but such deep openness usually takes years.

It's What You Notice

You walk past one another and let your fingers connect and gently linger before walking your separate ways. Later, his hands grab your waist and you sway in unison as you stir dinner on the stove while chaos from your boisterous family inevitably ensues. Yet you choose to notice only each other. You lock eyes, knowingly, remembering the flirtatious texts you sent while he was at the office all day. It's these small, continual efforts that act as the heartbeat of your love. Affection combined with connection, drenched in authentic communication, is the real secret to an intimate marriage.

— **Sondra Knight**, wife, mother, and home educator,
Lake Worth, Florida

Conquering Fear

Perhaps the biggest roadblock to real intimacy is the fear of revealing something that the other will mock or reject entirely. Though a different level of intimacy, this is true of friendship, as well. We might fear landing at the bottom of the heap, not being chosen or acknowledged. The acronym, FOMO (Fear of Missing Out), has become common in our age of digital interaction, and is often associated as a motivating factor to keep up with social media.

Opportunity for intimacy is often squandered because of fear. In a world of uncertainty and rapid change, how do we overcome fear? Faith is so essential. In 1 John 4:18 (WEB), the disciple reminds us that, "Perfect love casts out fear." Love stomps on fear, removes it from the picture and totally overcomes it. Love actively casts out fear. We must take an active step to simply let it go anytime it comes creeping up to the front door of our relationships. The power of love to overcome fear is manifest in the perfection of our holy, triune God. Dutch priest, theologian, and author Henri Nouwen discusses this perfection, pointing to the three-in-one source of love:

> When St. John says that fear is driven out by perfect love, he points to a love that comes from God, a divine love. He does not speak about human affection, psychological compatibility, mutual attraction, or deep interpersonal feelings. All of that has its value and beauty, but the perfect love about which St. John speaks embraces and transcends all feelings, emotions, and passions. The perfect love that drives out all fear is the divine love in which we are invited to participate.[9]

Such is the intimate communion we can have with God.

Intimacy is an invitation. God starts it. The very basis for relationship comes from God's triune nature. God eternally exists in the communion of the Father, Son, and Holy Spirit.[10] Love's source is the Father; Jesus came to make clear its way; the Holy Spirit is one who brings counsel and comfort. God calls out to us from the fellowship in the godhead and draws us into the ongoing relationship with Him. He reaches out to us but won't force us to love Him. Human intimacy echoes this, but we'll never do it perfectly. Only His love is perfect, and it's in Him that we find the bravery to step into the deep waters of intimacy with another living soul. As we find our place of belonging in Christ, we're better able to provide deep assurance to another as well as receive the acceptance needed to build a life of intimate relationships. Understanding that we're accepted in the Beloved is so much a part of the "house of relationship."[11]

Passionate, intimate relationships require us to reckon with the fear of being open, moving past it so love can deepen. Nouwen describes it well:

> Intimacy is not found on the level where fear resides. Intimacy is not a happy medium. It is a way of being in which the tension between distance and closeness is dissolved and a new horizon appears. Intimacy is beyond fear. Those who have experienced the intimacy to which Jesus invites us no longer need to worry about getting too close or becoming too distant. When Jesus says: 'Do not be afraid; it is I,' he reveals a new space in which we can move freely without fear. This intimate space is not a fine line between distance and closeness, but a wide field of movement in which the question of whether we are close or distant is no longer the guiding question.[12]

Regardless of gender, financial situation, or communication skills, the field is open for us all, no matter the season of life. If intimacy is available, the question then remains, "How much do I desire intimacy in my life?" Or "Am I willing to take the next step in openness and begin to build trust?"

Conclusion

In this chapter I've looked at aspects of relationships that most impact intimacy. I've shown how passion, openness, and stretching past our personal comfort zones help us develop and maintain close relationships. I've addressed the importance of overcoming fear, building trust over time, and discovered how the possibility for intimate relationships increases as we give control to God, trusting Him with the precious people in our lives. Whether it's friendship or family life, moving in the steady rhythm of open communication and the goodness of God's love creates a solid foundation for relationships that thrive.

In the next chapter I'll look at some of the ways conflict can hamper such fruitful thriving, and what to do about it. Learning to apologize when we've done wrong or made less than loving decisions is a start, but reconciliation takes more than simply saying "I'm sorry."

Questions for Reflection

1. Control and trust are two elements of intimacy discussed in this chapter. Which one do you have the most trouble with and why?

2. What is it about passion that can be confusing? Why?

3. Were there days in the past when you felt more comfortable being open with a friend? If so, describe those days in your journal. Remind yourself what was happening and how you felt during that time.

Chapter 9

Working through Relational Conflict

All this is from God, who reconciled us to Himself through Christ, and gave us the ministry of reconciliation.
— 2 Corinthians 5:18, NIV

FRANK, THE MAN you adore, refuses to discuss his continual tendency to lie. You believe he loves you, too, but he is completely closed to discussing the differences between you.

No matter how hard we try to bring balance and peace to our relationships, if one person in a relationship ignores or pulls away, there's little hope for healing. Right? Not exactly. Conventional wisdom says that "it takes two" for a relationship to flourish but there are ways to keep key relationships sound even without both parties sharing the same dedication to strong, healthy communication. If we sharpen our own communication, we might bring forth fruit with even the most wayward of lovers or friends.

But resolving conflict takes more than being an active listener, a good conversationalist, or spending enough time in each other's presence. There was a period when my best friend ditched me and wouldn't speak to me for about ten years. Worse yet, she wouldn't tell me what I might have done wrong and kept assuring me she wasn't angry. She just needed a break, she said. Our children were each other's closest companions, spending all their time playing together while she and I shared, cried, and commiserated during our years of young motherhood. Along with dishes that needed to be washed, carpets that needed to be vacuumed, and a myriad of other kid-chaos, we met several times weekly over tuna salad sandwiches, pickles, and chips. We were more like sisters. Then, suddenly, she pulled away.

My emotions ran from utter befuddlement and hurt to outrage. How could she do this to me? To the children? Thankfully, I was blessed with many other lovely friends, some just as close. But people aren't exchangeable parts. Her exit left a major gap in my life. Years later, we reconnected at a funeral. She explained her odd behavior over a decade before and apologized with tears. She openly explained the alienation and pain she had been experiencing years earlier. But I was unsettled. I'd already forgiven her in my own mind and heart. When it was apparent that she wasn't just going through a phase, I grieved the loss, forgave her, and (sadly) let her go. No longer would I allow her rejection to live rent-free in my head. Eventually, our friendship was restored, but it took almost five more years to regain trust and renewed closeness. When I finally was able to lay down my guard, we wept and laughed our way back to a full and flourishing friendship.

Friends, siblings, couples, and all relationships have deeply spiritual dimensions, requiring steady doses of forgiveness. When there's been a breach of trust or a major conflict and we say, "It's all good," or "No problem," the relationship often suffers from lack of dealing with the underlying issues. Serious work needs to be done to process relational conflicts and conundrums. Fruits of the Spirit (see Gal. 5:22–23) such as perseverance and self-control will strengthen us and will also help us keep conflict from ruining our relationships. This is because God is in the business of knitting hearts together and bringing reconciliation. But if we bury the problems, we keep His hand away from helping us. It's important to remember that God is with us in whatever conflict may exist, ready to lead, guide, and bring us through the deep, often turbulent waters of conflict. One of my favorite Psalms says, "Even though I walk through the darkest valley, I will fear no evil for you are with me" (Ps. 23:4, NIV). Even without immediate relief from the darkest conflict, there's hope for change. He is with us.

The first step in overcoming differences always starts with us. That's the most challenging part. The easy part is that even if our spouse, friend, co-worker, or sibling is unwilling to deal with conflict, we're never out there on our own without help or comfort. Quaker missionary Thomas Kelly writes: "From our end of the relationship [we] can send out eternal love in silent, searching hope and meet each person with a background of eternal expectation and a silent, wordless prayer of love."[1] Prayer is central for resolving conflict. I'll explore its place more fully in coming chapters. For now, I'll focus on the connection between conflict and forgiveness, especially how God's grace and His call to humility address conflict. I'll then dig into how relationship talk can foster relational repair. We must be willing to confront conflict head-on. Our digitally saturated environment and pervasive popular culture complicate these challenges.

The book of Lamentations reminds us how the ancient Hebrews responded as Judah (Israel's southern kingdom) was besieged by Nebuchadnezzar. Their holy city was facing disaster, but the Hebrews remained hopeful instead of giving in to despair: "But this I call to mind, and therefore I have hope: The steadfast love of the Lord never ceases, his mercies never come to an end; they are new every morning; 'great is your faithfulness'" (Lam. 3:21–23, ESV). Hope within ruin is seen all throughout the scriptures. God's work of mercy, grace, and forgiveness is the perfect environment for resolving conflict, no matter how great.

Communicating Grace through Forgiveness

Relational inaccuracies and false beliefs are the prime culprits in messing up our relationships. When I engage in relationship coaching, I deal with such inaccuracies and false beliefs right away. "It's all good" is an example. Life isn't all good and pretending it is doesn't make the pain go away. God's grace is available to each of us but extending grace to a friend or our spouse doesn't mean that we bury the conflict in the sand, pretend it didn't happen or somehow convince ourselves that the offense doesn't matter.

Grace, as a posture toward others, allows us to respond carefully, taking time to measure words and actions instead of reacting emotionally in ways that damage relationships. Grace is a quality that suggests beauty and poise. A graceful person is stable, steady, and agile. Think of a dancer, holding her position on the high bar, capable, strong, and well-disciplined. That posture did not come overnight. It was attained with ease because it became part of the rhythm of the dancer's life, and because she has practiced for years. Someone who is full of grace can respond to another with kindness when conflict arises, rather than immediately reacting in defense of self. Grace tempers our attitude. Grace has its source in the love of God. The Apostle Paul explains this to the young Ephesian believers, when he writes it "is by grace you have been saved, through faith—and this is not from yourselves, it is the gift of God" (Eph. 2:8, NIV).

Two Good Forgivers

In a world where too many marriages don't last longer than a breath mint, what's the key to longevity in marriage? What's the key to staying close? Billy Graham once remarked about the key to a long-lasting marriage: "It is comprised of Two Good Forgivers."[2]

Forgiving freely is a critical element in loving your spouse; in fact, it isn't an option if we want to stay out of divorce court!

Good forgivers know these basic forgiveness maxims:

1. To forgive is a heroic choice, and it's not for the weak but the strong.

2. To daily forgive one another for what we do best—be human—which is often messy.

3. Being offended is inevitable but staying offended is a choice.

4. If I go to bed angry with my spouse, I will wake up a little less in love with them.

5. Being a good forgiver and a good lover are inextricably linked.

6. Couples who struggle to forgive each other are the norm, but God freely forgave us in Jesus so that we could freely forgive each other.

My marriage has lasted 48 years because my husband and I have applied these maxims.

— **Jackie Kendall**, author of *Free Yourself to Love: The Liberating Power of Forgiveness*

In the biblical sense, then, grace is much more than poise, elegance, or the result of personality types. It's an unmerited favor. Essentially, grace is favor. It's acceptance that's given to another even when it's undeserved. Just as the Father lavishes His grace on us daily, so too can we let grace flow to others. Sometimes grace will mean we're patient and quiet. At other times it means we reserve judgement and give someone the benefit of the doubt. If we long for lasting love in all our relationships, God's grace to us is essential. Professor and author Quentin Schultze says, "Apart from grace, all our communication tends toward symbolic entropy. It simply falls apart."[3]

The need for grace is clear when conflict is growing. Communicating lovingly in respectful, kind, and patient ways during conflict can bring healing when fellowship is broken. The practice of loving, grace-filled communication is a balm for the soul that works double-duty; first, by making room for the relationship to deepen, and second, by providing a path toward lasting reconciliation.

Maintaining a strong faith in God doesn't free us from all the frailties and gut-wrenching emotions associated with our broken humanness. Whether in friendship or romance, faith shows us ways to communicate our love despite the hurts or rifts we experience. Faith directs us to kindness, a charge given to us by the Apostle Paul: "Be ye kind and compassionate to one to another, forgiving one another just as in Christ God forgave you" (Eph. 4:32, NIV).

Everyone who has been hurt knows it's a challenge to forgive. God directs us how and when to do so, by the power of the Holy Spirit. But we still must learn how He does this, especially what He requires of us.

Retelling the Story

Simply quoting chapter and verse is no more than spiritual bypassing, and that doesn't bring healing, just a deeper rut. We must learn how to actually forgive and that means looking at the offense head-on, calling it what it is, and then letting go of the hurt. This act of forgiveness is a process that involves replacing negative narratives about others with a new, redemptive story. That's what I did with my estranged friend during our early parenting years. Even though she refused to talk with me, I began seeing her in the story of God's grace.

Over time, I started to see her the way God did as a loving, forgiving Father. It's one thing to decide to forgive an offense, but without acknowledging and then releasing the emotional pain associated with the offense the relationship will never truly be restored. I released her to God's hands. Communication professors Jonathan Pettigrew and Diane Badzinski describe this process as "an internal change of heart toward a person who was unfair."[4] This measure of forgiveness involves seeing the other with eyes of kindness—choosing, in a sense, to view the other as one who would offer the same to us.

The charge to be kind doesn't demand agreement. Even if the other person is completely to blame, or if conflict stems from the frustration of being misunderstood, it's possible to put the other first and consider his feelings and needs. Relating in this way requires a depth of love and a deep commitment to the relationship even when the other person isn't present. We talk kindly about the other person to ourselves and to God, hoping for the opportunity to continue that dialogue of grace with the other person. This kind of communication is known as *relationship talk*.

Relationship Talk

Relationship talk defines the relationship (DTR) and helps maintain it by tracking the changing needs and feelings of the other. Students at my university in Florida use the DTR acronym as well-known code when discussing each other's relationship status. In fact, walking along the intracoastal waterway near campus is "the" place where couples define their relationship, typically moving from friends to dating or dating to exclusivity. Once the relationship has been defined, relationship talk continues the conversation.[5] While such relationship talk is almost solely associated with romantic relationships, friends may find a similar type of relationship talk helpful when building trust and vulnerability.[6] This type of meta-communication (or communicating about the relationship) is an effective and valuable way to continue growing close instead of drifting apart. Even after three or thirty years of marriage, couples need regular relationship talk. When a couple has a daily or weekly opportunity to talk about their relationship, it establishes a foundation for the two to communicate about change before arguing or breaking apart. Establishing a regular rhythm of relationship talk helps to steer couples clear of relationship pitfalls.

When relationship talk is drenched in grace and heavily sprinkled with openness, honesty, and trust, it sets the tone to give one another the benefit of the doubt. Dealing with everyday conflict necessitates giving another this benefit. When trust has been broken, especially if it's reoccurring, it's a greater challenge to keep stepping up to healthy relationship talk and give someone the benefit of the doubt. Instead of addressing the situation at hand, we're apt to pull away or to blurt out the most mean-spirited accusations, most of which we truly don't even mean but are the result of unresolved wounds and offenses. These quick, thoughtless reactions worsen the conflict, delay reconciliation, and sometimes destroy the relationship.

Before graduate school, I worked in the wedding industry as lead singer and manager of a band called Radiance. For almost twenty years, my husband and I played music for many couples' first dance. The many wedding receptions in which we performed taught me a lot, but what stands out most is that no one gets married expecting that they'll eventually divorce. Rather, people always hope it will work out. One of the smartest ways to nurture that desire is to set aside a regular time to communicate every day. I often wonder how many of even the most apparently Christian couples practice relationship talk. It doesn't have to be something formal or heavy. You may simply say, "How are you feeling today?" or "What's happening at work?"

Easy divorce became prominent in the 1970s and 1980s in America and hasn't let up much since then. What seems like good news is a report by the Institute for Family Studies revealing that divorce in America is trending downward. However, so is the institution itself. Marriage rates are decreasing, and it appears that as an institution less of the population are choosing it.[7] Instead, sharing a bed and simply living together has become increasingly the norm. The gap between true love and illusion appears to be growing in almost every sector of life and is perhaps most readily observed in what's produced in popular culture.

Broken hearts are plentiful today, but they're not a one-size-fits-all phenomenon. Children can shatter their parents' hearts. A father can devastate the heart of his son or daughter. Friends can surely break our hearts. When we walk in any of these close relationships there will be times when we don't agree or times when one has wronged the other. Here, grace-filled relationship talk is invaluable. Without it, there is little room for forgiveness and renewal.

The Influence of Popular Music

Popular music both shapes and reflects our relationships. Countless songs teach us lies about love. Like toddlers learn the alphabet by singing their ABCs, we absorb the lines of love's fantasy with catchy tunes. The ideas become imprinted in our brains. So many of these songs speak of broken hearts left in the wake of unresolved conflict. They powerfully remind us of the ache for true love and how hard it is to find. The melodies and rhythms of popular music become embedded in our subconscious mind.

For example, Beyonce's 2016 song "Sandcastles" emits sadness through every mournful note. She complains about relational conflict as it remains unresolved. She sings about dishes that are smashed on the counter and picture frames that have been emptied of their family photos. Her lyrics touch something deep in the hearts of her listeners: the familiar ache of the broken-hearted.[8]

Past musical generations are similar. In 1989, singer/songwriter Vonda Shepherd released a song called "Baby, Don't You Break My Heart Slow." This pop ballad tells another story of relational ruin. In it, Shepherd laments the broken promises and illusions of romantic love.[9]

More recently, Taylor Swift, *Time Magazine's* "Person of the Year" made millions revealing her own broken heart through her music.[10] When I consider some of the lyrics to her blockbuster hit, "The Best Day," it nearly brings me to tears thinking about how much it can hurt to be rejected by people we call friends. Swift's personal heartache reportedly goes a bit like this: as a middle-schooler, the future pop star called each of her closest friends one Saturday and invited them to go to the mall with her.[11] One by one they declined with something else to do that day. But when Swift decided to go by herself, she saw all those friends there together. They had intentionally left her out. Her lyrics tap into the pain she felt that day.

Writing a song, listening to it, and singing the song may be cathartic, but healing is found as we lean into the loving arms of God and learn to find comfort there. The Psalmist wrote, "the Lord is close to the broken hearted and saves those who are crushed in spirit" (Ps. 34:18, NIV). Songs that resonate with so many couples may provide a medium for lament, but they also echo the of emptiness in failing to express what a healthy romantic relationship looks like.

Music's major influence in public perception of love began long before Taylor Swift, Vonda Shepherd, or Beyonce. Early in the last century, the innocent, catchy tunes of the 1950s, 1960s, and 1970s captured the pain of broken hearts just as readily as today's songs. One earlier hit song was a lilting melody from 1972 sung by Roberta Flack and Donny Hathaway. The wistful voices of this soulful duet put a probing question to melody, begging audiences to listen. "Where is the Love?" provided audiences with mournful questions about the unreality of love, leaving listeners dangling without answers.

Taylor Swift's 2010 melodramatic "Last Kiss" tells a familiar breakup story. Swift describes herself sitting on the floor in misery, wearing her boyfriend's clothes, unable to imagine how their relationship ended.[12] These feelings and experiences aren't new, but are today complicated with the angst of one-night hook-ups and even fewer examples of what commitment to a relationship even looks like.

Popular music has a long history of producing deeply felt music surrounding the pain of break ups and relational conflict. For example, Simon and Garfunkel's blockbuster hit from the 1960s, *Bridge Over Troubled Water*, topped the charts for many months. The title brings up a mental image of the need to bridge the gap between love and conflict. So many relationships crumble without that bridge. The song points to the brokenness that comes from the inability (or unwillingness) to brave the choppy waters and deal with conflict.

Surely the sorry state of so many marriages and friendships doesn't stem solely from the illusions presented by pop music stars, but they do possess a potent recipe to persuade, teach, and entertain. That trifecta has sent many potentially strong relationships into the trash heap.

Resolving Conflict

Multiple factors contribute to truncated, fractured relationships, but one is at the top of the list: unresolved conflict. One key to keeping the door of love open is learning to address conflict instead of wishing it away or pretending it doesn't exist. In the theme verse for this chapter, 2 Corinthians 5:18, the Apostle Paul taught the early Christians about God's work of reconciliation through the cross. He broadened their understanding of this essential element of life, explaining that we're all a part of the ministry of reconciliation. In his New Testament letter, James addresses the reason for conflict, "What causes fights and quarrels among you? Don't they come from your desires that battle within you?" (Jas. 4:1, NIV).

Emphasizing grace in conflict resolution is a helpful, instant reminder of our own potential culpability. This is of utmost importance in our relationships, especially when we're in the middle of conflict. Establishing a posture of grace means that we make room for others' personality quirks, imperfections, and areas of struggle. It means we believe in another and make room for him as he is, imperfections and all. Cynics may criticize such an underlying attitude and advise against it so one can avoid being disappointed. But love continually looks for ways to encourage and uplift others, and grace is the necessary ingredient that will keep relationships flourishing. Understanding grace helps us to forgive another's offenses and keep relationships alive.

Conflict may involve lengthy dispute, simple controversy, a difference of opinion, or a sharp clash in what's perceived as acceptable behavior. It may be brought on by choosing the wrong words to express yourself, an ongoing disagreement over style or belief, or a simple facial expression such as a raised eyebrow. Often conflict creates a quarrel; sometimes the sad result is a broken relationship.

Conflict doesn't have to end in relational ruin. Sometimes, ongoing conflict isn't so much a problem with the person with whom we're relating, but it's a matter of broken communication, a "blockage."[13] When communication is blocked, it must be opened up, not ignored or forgotten. This requires intentional reconciliation. To reconcile with another requires communication skills and the will to see beyond the conflict to healing. Restoration of affection, harmony, and strength is the result of successful reconciliation. When the doors to reconciliation seem completely shut, there is a path to follow that's counterintuitive, but it's the necessary salve.

To communicate love or affection effectively we'll have to learn how to travel together through unstable terrain. Just as the landscape changes depending upon where we're on the globe, the seasons and settings of our primary relationships are always changing. There will be mountains, valleys, rocks, stones, rivers, hills, and perhaps even some caverns as we journey through life with others. But if we see this uneven landscape as an adventure, we'll find strength along the way. In restorative communication "we open the door for another by humbling ourselves."[14]

Humility

Humility is perhaps the most underrated element of relationship talk. Without it, conflict seems to multiply like weeds in an untended garden. Humility and grace don't just walk side-by-side; they walk hand-in-hand. If we think we're impervious to sin, temptation, mistakes, or even downright ugly behavior, it's much more difficult to extend grace to others. But knowing that the source of the problem could be "me" is probably the most important feature humility brings into any relationship. Even seemingly minor but unresolved issues can undermine strong relationships.

Restoring the sacred trust of a relationship involves a willingness to humble oneself and make it a daily priority to keep a clean slate. Humility may not be the most glamorous guest at love's table, but it must be a welcome one. The humility of Christ is evident all throughout Scripture. The Apostle Paul told the early church: "Therefore, as God's chosen people, holy and dearly loved, clothe yourselves with compassion, kindness, humility, gentleness and patience" (Col. 3:12, NIV). A strong dose of such humility is an absolute necessity in the process of resolving conflict, and an essential element of true love.

Conflict tests a relationship's determination. Will you get through it to the other side? Will hurt feelings and raw emotion take the lead, or will forgiveness and reconciliation win the day? Thomas Merton explains the testing that occurs in every relationship: "The purest faith has to be tested by silence in which we listen for the unexpected, in which we're open to what we don't yet know, and in which we slowly and gradually prepare for the day when we will reach out to a new level of being with God."[15] Although Merton discusses the importance of waiting patiently for a new level of being with God, the same may be applied to being with a friend, spouse, sister or brother. True, deep, mature love takes time. Love gets better as it ages.

The Bible includes a wealth of wisdom about reducing conflict. Whether we're dealing with a friend or lover we learn that a "gentle answer turns away wrath, but a harsh word stirs up anger. The tongue of the wise adorns knowledge, but the mouth of the fool gushes folly" (Prov. 15:1–2, NIV). Paul tells us to avoid letting the sun go down while we're still angry.[16] He doesn't say that we'll never be angry or upset, but that we shouldn't let even one day go by without addressing these feelings.

Confrontation

Most of us don't like to confront conflict. When a friend or spouse doesn't reciprocate with healing words or even the openness necessary to confront an issue, it may be a great challenge to remain loving. But it's important to remember that just because someone is unable (or unwilling) to articulate her feelings, it doesn't mean she doesn't love you. Perhaps your husband is unable to manage the pain or disappointment he feels about the loss of his father and would rather not talk about it. Maybe your wife's coping skills are weak. Or a trusted friend who is normally quite transparent may not want to discuss something she has yet to resolve; perhaps she fears your rejection or is simply in too much inner turmoil to articulate her problem. There are many reasons why we shut down. No matter what words we choose to help restore the relationship, the one we love might remain closed. We might need prayer coupled with active kindness and attention.

Yet, confrontation is important. It's better not to let argumentation become a norm, for bouncing back from a fight with a friend, neighbor, or loved one isn't easy. It sometimes takes years to build back a sense of trust and affection after a fiery disagreement or headstrong clash. However, even if strong words end up being said in haste, it's better to confront than to ignore the conflict. Otherwise, conflict will continue to stir up the waters and the relationship will continually be in a state of risk. Above all, don't ignore those who aren't ready or able to confront. Perhaps time to cool off is necessary. Giving someone the silent treatment doesn't get rid of the problem; it simply dismisses the person. This kind of silence doesn't foster healing; it rejects the person. Even when the intent isn't to reject, the silent treatment sure feels that way.

Along with emotional distress, immediate practical issues must be dealt with when there is conflict. A common example in the world of room-mates is leaving the dishes in the sink. One friend likes to have a clean, neat kitchen. The other doesn't care much about it and might be happy washing the dishes every two or three days. Or neighbors may disagree over who will pay for the new shared fence. One demands a fence but claims no responsibility for the cost because it runs along the other's property line. Such situations may start out as a menial bit of neighborhood business and end up in a territorial war. As a result, neighborliness vanishes, replacing warmth and familiarity with a cold chill. When my best friend cut me out of her life years ago, I felt legitimate anger, but I had to get to a place of letting that anger go and forgiving her. I had a choice whether to hold a grudge or to bring it to the feet of Jesus and trust the Lord for healing. When we finally took steps back to each other there was plenty of time to talk about what happened. We discussed our differences. We opened our hearts to reconciliation, and we've been reunited ever since.

Conclusion

Humility, grace, and forgiveness all work together to help us overcome conflict and walk in the freshness and beauty of reconciliation.[17] The work of growing relationships that move beyond conflict to flourishing involves effort and intentionality. Beyond intentionality, a strong deposit of emotional resilience is required. The ability to rally oneself and regain emotional fortitude is essential. In some ways this may be easier in a marriage where the couple has become accustomed to each other's ways. But strong or weak, the question is the same for all relationships: How do we bounce back, adapt to change, and get past a conflict? This is a process that involves a different aspect of relational soundness. From forgiveness and reconciliation, we must move to repair. Repairing a relationship is as unique and complex as each unique individual friendship or marriage. It's a willingness to continue talking, praying, and working out the feelings involved that ultimately moves us to repair.

Questions for Reflection

1. How might you address everyday conflict through grace, humility, and open communication? Choose one and explore the way it might provide a healing salve to a current relationship.

2. What part of relationship talk is most challenging for you to think about and why?

3. What part of the reconciliation process is confusing or most difficult for you (acknowledging everyday conflict, extending grace, confronting the chaos, etc.), and why?

Chapter 10

Addressing Chaos in Relationships

For all of you who were baptized into Christ have clothed yourselves with Christ.

— Galatians 3:27, NIV

IT'S MOVING DAY. Just when you think you've got the van unloaded and all
the endless boxes nicely stacked from wall-to-wall in your new place, you
turn and see the oversized sofa. There it sits, large, lumbering, and cozy in
the green grass, mostly hidden on the other side of the moving van. Luckily,
a couple of your strongest friends have stuck around and you quickly ask for
their help to move just one more thing. One look at the enormous piece of
furniture and they know there's going to be some immediate heavy lifting.

Isn't it like this when a marriage or friendship has been through a
long haul of conflict or a major breach in fidelity, and the longing for rest
and normalcy is within sight? Why is it then that you find yourselves doing
some of the heaviest lifting of your relationship? During such times it's important to remember that anything worth doing is going to take consistent
effort. Giving up isn't an option; you've come too far.

In this chapter, I address relationships that need deep work, those
that are beyond occasional conflicts or petty arguments. Some of our relationships are so deeply broken that they may seem irreparable. Finding
our way back to each other involves everything we already know about
forgiveness, grace, and strong communication skills, but then requires
what many therapists call "doing the work" of repair.

In the pages ahead we'll explore some of the common mistakes associated with healing this dysfunctional way of being in a relationship
and seek to understand how to repair the breeched walls of your sacred
circle, beloved family, or precious friendship. First, I review the basics of
relational maintenance, the "Three C's" of consideration, confession, and
communion. Then, I explore several practical safeguards for the upkeep of
your relationships. These include feeling our feelings, being attentive to the
stories we tell ourselves, and using respectful language.

115

The Three C's

Three little "C" words make a world of difference. Each contributes to our ability to communicate love: consideration, confession, and communion.

Consideration

Consideration may be the easiest one to miss. It sounds so simple. If we can start each day with a willingness and intention to be considerate of those we're in a relationship with, then we set the tone for a loving day. Simple consideration creates mutual positive regard for healthy relationships. It's also, of course, appropriate to be considerate with everyone we meet, but so often we're better at being respectful and considerate to those we're not close to, neglecting our closer relationships.

Sometimes even silly things keep us from being considerate: a time crunch, oversleeping, and unforeseen delays are common. But hidden self-focus might lurk in the background; it's so easy to think only of ourselves. To be considerate means that we consider others. It means keeping each other in the decision-making processes for such things as plans, schedules, and purchases. Next is confession. Most of us don't relish the act of apology because admitting wrong doesn't feel good. We like to think we just made a little mistake or overlooked something rather than offended, but sometimes we fail, and sometimes we fail in a big way. The Apostle Paul offers no slack when advising the young Philippian Christians on related matters in the gathered assembly. He writes:

> Let this mind be in you, which was also in Christ Jesus, who being in the form of God did not consider it robbery to be equal with God, but made Himself of no reputation, taking the form of a bondservant and coming in the likeness of men. And, being found in appearance as a man, He humbled Himself and became obedient to the point of death, even the death of the cross. (Phil. 2:5–8, NKJV)

Like today, Jesus's humility was completely opposite of the prominent attitudes among first-century people. Humility infers lowliness, a posture that we like to avoid. Humility sounds like the attitude of a weak person, a deficit in one's personality rather than a strength. But the humble person is strong and servant oriented. Humility breaks the bonds of arrogance and stubbornness associated with unhealthy relationships.

Confession

Humility also sets the scene for *confession*: I did wrong. I failed you. I hurt you, I am sorry. Whether the confession is over a small mistake or a major one, remaining humble leads to greater consideration and deepening love.[1] Humility opens a window to greater peace and harmony. When two people are considerate of each other's needs and desires, the room for offense shrinks dramatically. Paul emphasized this dynamic when he said, "Let nothing be done through selfish ambition or conceit, but in lowliness of mind let each esteem others better than himself. Let each of you look out not only for his own interests, but also for the interests of others" (Phil. 2:3–4, ESV).

Although Paul was writing to the Church, specifically speaking about relationships among brothers and sisters in Christ, his words serve all relationships. Part of this posture of humility is in the acknowledgment and confession that must come before an apology is offered. A vague sort of "I'm sorry that you feel that way," doesn't work. Or "I'm sorry for everything; I'll do better." What are you sorry for? What specifically did you do that hurt your friend? How did you let him down? Making confession a regular part of everyday life goes a long way toward setting the pace for effective, healthy, loving interaction.

Communion

Consideration and confession pave the way for *communion*. Communion is a beautiful picture of what it means to live in harmony, peace, and to experience relationships that flourish. Although there are numerous levels of coming into union with another, I believe communion is a matter of spiritual closeness, and is part of the experience the early disciples had with Jesus and each other. It's not the sexual one-flesh relationship of husband and wife, but the kind of oneness Jesus taught. In John's telling of the Gospel, Jesus's prayer to the Father was that "they may be one, even as I and Thou are one" (John 17:20–22, NIV). Jesus prays for his disciples to walk in communion.[2]

Such communion is beyond words. The work of relational repair is one stop along the way to true reconciliation and eventually communion, or a true oneness with the other. If consideration, confession, and communion are lacking in the face of major relational hurdles, it's probably time to get some outside help such as therapy, counseling, or some focused conversation with a safe and trusted friend who is impartial to the situation. Therapy can help. Many people avoid therapy because they perceive it as an indicator of a failed relationship. They perceive the work ahead as something that they should be able to handle themselves. But saying yes to therapy means the relationship is worth the time, money, and energy. Don't be afraid to ask for help.

I repeat: When a marriage needs repair, sometimes it's best to seek the impartiality of a good therapist. A wise therapist can see things that we would miss. They are often able to give the gentle nudge needed to deal squarely with cyclical or major problematic issues. This is key because so much relational conflict is the result of very small, barely significant issues that become large and eventually results in bitterness. Feelings and resentments are often hidden. When unaddressed, they grow, and mistrust of the other's intentions begin to take root.

Some issues can be corrected by steady, intentional face-to-face communication, but some are big ones that need major outside help. When trust is broken it takes a lot to build it back. This may be especially true when dealing with verbal or physical abuse, and infidelity which can keep even the most patient people stuck in relational misery for years.[3] Talking about any unfaithfulness is essential for regaining relational communion. It's a key part of processing pain. However, without a doubt, talking isn't enough. Forgiveness is another key. It's always part of the recovery process. Still, it's easy to apologize and yet remain stuck in the cycle of hurting one another.

Can a couple (or a friendship) truly bounce back to a renewed and refreshed close relationship after a major rupture? Sometimes only the people involved in the relationship can dismantle the false structures. Such false structures involve the rhythms and rituals of a relationship, the external ways of being together rather than the heart of love and care within us. Many times, false structures are more like children's "tinker toys." Once a piece or two are removed, the entire structure collapses and we realize we've been tiptoeing across scaffolding instead of the sturdy floor and ground of relationship. Without addressing false structures, the issues remain and taunt us. Despite the desire to maintain a relationship, the answers largely depend on the willingness of both parties to persevere through the many varieties of heartache. The work of relational repair is much deeper than simply resolving a conflict. Both communication skills and willingness are important to ongoing relationships, but it's a bit like the difference between having a sprained ankle and being in a full body cast.

The restored friendship I mentioned in the last chapter involved the full-body-cast type of rift. That friendship was gone, grieved, and buried. When restoration came it was more like the resurrection of Lazarus. The first few years we spent unraveling the graveclothes; our intermittent and brief conversations ploughed the ground for spending time together again, but in the deepest places of my soul I never imagined I could ever trust her again. Part of the problem was my own level of pain. Throughout our twenties our young children spent nearly every day together. When she pulled away from me, she also pulled her children away from mine. Yet here we are, 15 years later and our friendship is stronger than it's ever been. This is due to the grace of God and the work of relational repair. There was some mighty heavy lifting to do as well as the miraculous, lavish grace of God pouring out on us as we made our way back to each other.

Doing the Work

Moving into true relational repair is a type of "doing the work," much akin to the challenging inner reflection and discipline taught in the modern Recovery Movement. One arm of the movement—Alcoholics Anonymous—has continued successfully for over 50 years to help individuals repair relationships. The organization has small recovery groups throughout the U.S. and the world, helping people regain their lives from the stranglehold of various addictions.[4]

Although there are 12 steps in the recovery process, healing doesn't happen in easily ordered, sequential steps. First there must be an admission that the problem exists. From there, the work continues by the participants taking responsibility for their feelings, choices, and lifestyle. They must call on the help of their higher power. Those who walk in the freedom of their recovery from drugs, alcohol, or other addictions take stock of their part in their own relational ruptures and diligently begin to work on ways to make amends to those who have been hurt along the way. Once this foundational part of the process is earnestly embraced, incorporating several regular healthy practices can help. The recovery movement has much to teach us about relational health.

Instead of running away, placing blame completely on the other, or pretending the breach isn't serious, it's helpful to work through a process that includes: (1) acknowledging our feelings; (2) examining the stories we tell ourselves; and (3) using language that heals or hurts.

Acknowledging Our Feelings

Acknowledging our feelings requires giving some extra attention to what's within our inner landscape instead of the conflict that's going on interpersonally. What "baggage" do you carry from your past, whether consciously or subconsciously? Baggage means that each of us comes to a relationship carrying a load of unresolved experiences, pains, and problems. These may include trauma, abuse, or regular instability from the past that hold us back from healthy relationships today. These are parts of our experience that keep us from flourishing and can be anything from an absent father or mother to physical or sexual abuse, abandonment, severe poverty, being bullied, or any number of destabilizing experiences. It's often these tragic or traumatic experiences that shape our beliefs about our world and ourselves. To become free of the mental chatter and debilitating relational conundrums associated with these issues, we've got to learn how to stop stuffing our feelings and deal with them, no matter how difficult.

This is the strength of Robert S. McGee's work in his book *Search for Significance*. Attending to this work is what he calls, "taking a trip in."[5] It's there, within the most personal space of our inmost being, that we must confront the stories we tell ourselves and bring them into the light of God's love.

Examining the Stories We Tell Ourselves

Acknowledging past hurts helps us discern what stories we've told ourselves, stories that may or may not be true. This is essential when it comes to the work of repairing a relationship.

Uncovering the false beliefs we've adopted over the course of our lives is very much situated in the stories we tell ourselves.

For example, if you were the middle child in a family of seven you might feel invisible. You may have had wonderful, loving parents, but still remember that you felt lost within your siblings' needs. Death or terminal disease of a parent is another type of trauma, as is divorce. The pangs of physical or verbal abuse carry long lasting repercussions and are often the source of much insecurity. Without investigating those deep feelings of hurt and betrayal and working through them, our story won't change.

Like a caged tiger at the zoo, we may find ourselves walking in tiny circles of anger and resentment, stuck in the same relationship troubles. Dysfunction becomes the norm. The way to break free from such deep relational ruin is to acknowledge the feelings of being let down, disappointed, or even betrayed, thereby clearing a road toward recovery. This is just one of the many ways to call it out or to name it. The very act of naming the emotions we feel can break chains that have held us captive for years, so being honest with yourself is an essential step. In fact, honesty is paramount in the work of major repair. I call it 3XL honesty. Being an honest person isn't as simple as refraining from lying. We need to be honest with ourselves about ourselves, honest with God about ourselves, and honest with at least one other.

Aside from the fact that confession is good for the soul, repressing our feelings is a guarantee that they will bubble up in a new form. James 5:16 (ESV) says, "Therefore, confess your sins to one another and pray for one another, that you may be healed. The prayer of a righteous person has great power as it is working." In other words, our feelings might end up coming out sideways if we don't confess them to each other. Harshness, impatience, infidelity, annoyance over petty issues, even major arguments can find their way out into our relationships when we don't acknowledge past hurts and traumas.

Using Language that Heals or Hurts

The language we use to deal with these major issues involves our own inner dialogue about hurt feelings and pain. This may be the most challenging part of doing the work. First, using self-respectful language may involve completely relearning what's appropriate and what isn't. If you grew up in a family where parents screaming at each other during dinner was the norm, or listened to them make snide comments about each other, that behavior and language is likely deeply entrenched in you.

Second, most of us tend to keep these negative, shameful narratives to ourselves. We don't want to be perceived as neurotic or insecure, so we tell no one. Instead of blowing over, however, the underlying issues gather like clouds before a storm, growing darker and more ominous. These narratives stay stuck somewhere down deep inside, stirring in our soul just below the surface of our consciousness. It may feel more comfortable to put a lid on the internal sorrow, but learning to spot those behaviors and words that trigger disrespectful attitudes is part of the work that helps maintain healthy relationships.

Allowing ourselves to acknowledge our feelings and examine the stories we tell ourselves helps set the pace for relational communication that's healthy, life-giving, and long-lasting—so much of which is expressed through the interlacing of both words and actions. Laced through all of these expressions of love is the importance of using respectful words. When we're so familiar with someone we've known or lived with for years, it's easy to forget the importance of respect. But without everyday respect, love fades. Choosing words wisely, responding instead of reacting, taking a moment to understand the wider context of whatever issue is at hand—all these very small steps can help us build the habits of respect and love in our relationships.

At lunch, your good friend lets you know she and another friend are planning a trip abroad. Feeling left out, you may tell yourself that someone else has taken your place. There may be no other indication of declining affection in this otherwise close friendship, but an alternative story bubbles to the surface from deep within the murky, subconscious waters of the soul. It's a narrative that we've been telling ourselves to cover up, a fear or a wound that's never been dealt with from the past. This happens all the time.

Jenny, a married woman who says she doesn't need affection, consistently sends out don't touch me signals, all the while craving her husband's affection. For 15 years she's been telling herself she isn't a very affectionate person and doesn't need it much, but she is miserable, and so is her husband, Derek. Jenny and Derek are caught in a dysfunctional cycle of reacting to the stories they've projected upon each other. They know they love each other, but neither understands why their relationship is so unsatisfying. She has the long-standing habit of repressing the feeling of being unlovable, feelings she may have experienced because of a failed relationship or with parents who loved her but showed little affection. To cope, she started stuffing her feelings of being unlovable below the level of conscious thought. Jenny may not even know what sabotaged her efforts for a healthy relationship, but something caused her to put a lid on her need for affection. It often feels safer to live in the story we tell ourselves than risk rejection, infidelity, or another failed attempt at relationship. The story she tells herself started out as a coping device; now she's stuck in a cycle of self-sabotage. Layers of script, performance, and awkward movement keep Jenny from the acceptance, love, and belonging that she truly longs for.

It's easy to project our own feelings of inadequacy onto loved ones. We imagine what they're feeling or thinking instead of dealing with the real issue. When we're not in touch with our feelings, we can all too easily create a narrative that's opposite to what's actually happening. The stories we tell ourselves can sound like the following:

- She's given up on me.
- He is rejecting me.
- They don't like me anymore.
- I just don't fit in.
- Why didn't they ask me?

Each of these woeful tales exist in the context of needing to belong, desiring love, and wanting to be known. Perhaps one is more familiar to you than another. Often, these are thoughts and projections that stem from feelings of insecurity or unresolved issues. When they're not addressed, they keep cycling back into our relationships and our work of repair can easily be halted. These thoughts and projections are often left over from childhood or picked up along the way in a person's key developmental years. Regardless, they cause a wide gap between how we think about ourselves and what others think about us.

The stories we tell ourselves tend to underestimate the positive regard of others. Such tales train our brains to think we're forgotten, disliked, or simply "not enough."[6] Thinking negatively about ourselves is part of our inner dialogue. If not adjusted and changed, our negative self-talk leads us to sabotage our ability to maintain healthy relationships. This type of self-talk may keep us from repairing a relationship that has been damaged.

Watching Our Words

Instead of inner dialogue that puts us in a pit of despair, we need to practice using living words of life, not just with each other, but in our communication with ourselves, or intrapersonal communication. Words that help keep communication in relationships strong don't arise out of a vacuum but are situated in the way we think about life; how we perceive ourselves in the tone and content of our inner dialogue.[7]

As our words increasingly emerge from a place of security, a place of deep, inner grounding in Christ, the longing for a relationship deeper than surface-level is likely to increase. We sense the sacredness of life that our Maker entrusted to us. God's love and our language entwine. Respect, love, and faith are braided together to become a cord that's "not quickly broken." The relationship stands strong, kept in place securely no matter how windy the day.[8] After all, words both reveal and shape our attitudes. They help us express love and discover we're loved in return.

Avoiding nasty language on social media is important. Using encouraging, kind words throughout the day online and offline sets the tone for healthy relationships. Even one kind word can turn away anger or misunderstanding. The essence of love and the language used to express it contains a power that doesn't fade with the trends of social media or the ability to text each other throughout the day.

One way of thinking about relational communication is to use *living words*. These positive words are spoken and shared in the present moment. Living words are those that help us stay in the present and find meaning in the moment together.[9] Such language brings refreshment and new life to others and to ourselves. These are life-giving, relationship-affirming words. I like to think of exchanging our dark and deceiving narratives about ourselves with words of affirmation and encouragement. The more we practice using such positive expressions, the more natural it becomes to regulate our words, choosing those that encourage and affirm instead of blame and shame. Professor Corey Anton describes such expressions:

> Words surround and engulf us, and they can be set in a kind of re-
> lief only momentarily. Never mere figures against a background,
> living words are themselves a continuous backgrounding. They do
> not happen within situations as much as make situations possible;
> situations can be what they are only because of words. That's why
> the expression, 'we were in a conversation' makes good sense.[10]

We change positively by using words that are affirming and respectful, rather than accusatory and biting.

Conclusion

Moving day is always upon us. We always feel the need to unpack our internal baggage. Once upon a time the first humans used fig leaves to cover their nakedness. Today, we clothe ourselves with labels, accomplishments, credentials, material goods, a fancy social media presence, and every manner of false security. The good news is that we don't have to settle for a tired old story that we tell ourselves about ourselves. We can respect those with whom we are in relationship because they are God's children, created in His image and likeness.

As Christ-followers, there is no need to keep covering ourselves with fig leaves. God provides clothing that's eternal.[11] The need to protect ourselves doesn't adequately cover up deeper needs to feel safe, to belong, or to be worthy of love. Neither do these things define us. As we name them, we can shed them and let the truth of our identity in Christ clothe us.

Remembering to pause and respond rather than to react helps us address each other with respectful, living words. The gentle nudge, the quiet look, a thoughtful pause or touch all work together much like the ingredients in fresh dough blend and mix as we give it time to rise.

In this chapter, I've looked at some of the deeper issues surrounding relational repair. Learning to do the work is a very active and challenging step on the road to beautiful, life-giving relationships. Going forward, I'll look at several active steps toward communicating love in ways that don't always use words.

Questions for Reflection

1. Why do we misunderstand or misinterpret what others are saying and take it so personally? Give one example from your own life.

2. What does it mean to you to "do the work" necessary for relationship maintenance?

3. Select one of the ways to practice respectful communication and take some time this week to reflect upon those things you have kept bottled up inside you that cause you to do or say hurtful things to the ones you care about most. What positive practices can you put in place to help you grow respectful communication in your relationships?

Chapter 11

Finding Strength and Solace
in Solitude

Everyone should be quick to listen, slow to speak and slow to become angry.

— James 1:19b, NIV

"FERME LA BOUCHE!" This French phrase means "shut your mouth." My own dear mother used it often. She would utter it with a wide and engaging smile but the look in her eyes made sure I took it seriously. As one might imagine, "quiet down!" was a regular request in those early years, especially when driving a group of six children all under the age of nine to the supermarket, school, or church. Later in life my family would laugh about it, remembering it fondly. Mom's utterance reminds me that there is a time for every season, including "a time to be silent and a time to speak" (Eccl. 3:7, NIV). Of course, appropriate silence is hindered daily, not only by rowdy kids, but by you and me.

Silence isn't only a reprieve from the noisy world of contemporary life. Relationally speaking, silence can be powerful, even part of the power to heal. Our relationships would explode or implode if we didn't stop talking long enough to assess them. Time spent in quiet thought can help us avoid dozens of relational mistakes.

In this chapter I address the role of silence in relational communication and miscommunication. I tackle nonverbal communication as a relational language and look at reflective silence to make room for thoughtful responses to loved ones. I consider the importance of communication context in using and understanding silence. Finally, I examine silence as part of our meaning-making. Before diving into these aspects of silence, however, let's begin with the generative power of words, including our tendency to get the last one in.

The Place of Silence

Words are like arrows. Once they shoot out of our mouths there's no taking them back. So what happens after harsh or unkind words have been directed toward people we care about most? Let's face it, friends have rifts, couples have arguments, parents and children have discussions, but even when things have smoothed over it's hard to forget the verbal slings and spears that have been directed our way. There is a truly proactive way to avoid an argument in the first place, and that begins wrestling with silence.

For those who are in relationships with someone who is domineering or has a not so gentle voice, the suggestion to use silence may make us pause. What if someone is verbally abusive? In such cases, silence can be toxic. What if something must be said to set things right, like undoing nasty gossip that's been broadcast as truth? There are times to stand up and be heard.

Many of us must learn the proper balance between confronting an issue or remaining silent. For me, the image of wrestling sometimes works well. Holding your tongue in a looming argument can feel just like a take down in a wrestling ring. The opponent has you nearly pinned and everything in you is screaming "fight, win!" It's never easy to back away from this type of situation, but when we step away from exclamatory or annoying remarks and offer peace-filled silence instead, we open ourselves up to an entirely different way of addressing conflict.

I originally discovered this idea through Dietrich Bonhoeffer, a theologian whose life on this earth was snuffed out in a German prison camp for speaking against Hitler during World War II. Bonhoeffer wrote about living authentically in a closely-knit community of faith. He sought to address the problems associated with a state-run church and advocated for "religionless Christianity," a practice that sought to keep true to biblical faith and teach the church to express itself in humility as brothers and sisters in community. He addressed the needed change in quite practical ways. One way was what he called the "ministry of holding one's tongue."[1]

This unusual ministry calls for willful restraint of one's voice, using silence as a loving response to someone who is being unreasonable, selfish, rude, or otherwise offensive. Though the precise phrase isn't in the Bible, the concept appears throughout Scripture. Perhaps the most prominent example is in the book of Ecclesiastes which calls for a time to be silent and a time to speak.[2] John writes, "Whoever has ears, let them hear what the Spirit says to the churches" (Rev. 2:7, NIV). The focus of this type of silence is to wait until the other has "ears to hear" or has returned to a more reasonable state of mind.

Bonhoeffer saw voluntary silence as a form of grace and an important part of ministry. While we're often preoccupied with the desire to speak and be heard, the "ministry of silence" is a relational must. The opposite is our tendency to use words to justify ourselves.[3] As Bonhoeffer explains, "Silence and speech have the same inner correspondence and difference as do solitude and community. One does not exist without the other. Right speech comes out of silence and right silence comes out of speech."[4] In his mind, silence wouldn't necessarily create agreement or eliminate oppression, but could prevent further relational damage and do much to keep the community of faith strong.[5] Although Bonhoeffer's primary audience was young seminarians, this "ministry of holding one's tongue" could serve all people who closely live together or work together.

The Right to Have the Last Word

Sometimes silence may be the most appropriate response. Remaining quiet when we want to give someone a piece of our mind can be frustrating; however, giving up the need to have the last word often stops escalating conflict and creates an atmosphere of openness. After all, arguments can turn unpleasant. We say things we don't mean. We accuse others or are being accused by others. Holding our tongues may just prevent a relational war.

Yet we can fall into the trap of using silence as a weapon. As discussed in a previous chapter, the silent treatment is the worst. Ignoring someone we love or admire is almost always a mistake. Perhaps we learned this counterproductive tactic from our families of origin. Parents or siblings might have learned just how to lock someone out of their life in such an unhealthy, hurtful way. The silent treatment actually says, "I don't care about you. I wish you were not in my life."

Lighten Up!

When is it okay to "make light" of a situation? I think it's both an art form and a skill set when it comes to communication, especially in the context of those who matter the most—our families.

For my family, humor serves as a game-changer in how we face inevitable problems.

My wife and I have three sons. As such, we're regularly surrounded by excessively energetic levels of interaction that invite conflict. Amidst the daily chaos, humor has become a crucial tool to foster long-term, positive family dynamics. Its use has not only lightened the mood in tough circumstances but has often altered our way of experiencing life together. Scholars have explored the multifaceted benefits of humor in familial contexts. It acts as a social balm, easing tension and promoting open communication. Sharing laughter cultivates a sense of unity, creating healthy emotional and mental bonds that transcend challenges. Humor functions as a coping mechanism, enabling families to navigate adversities with resilience. While not a cure-all, humor can promote a positive family environment, fostering a culture of cohesion, playfulness, and joy. So don't just get through life, make fun of it, and laugh together as often as possible.

— **Joseph W. Sowers**, Assistant Professor of Communication, Palm Beach Atlantic University

The Power of Nonverbal Communication

While the power of silence as a nonverbal cue is evident, there are many other silent messages that are communicated with or without intention. We can intentionally wink at a friend or a loved one. Or we can just close our eyes, making our partner or friend wonder if we're sleepy, disinterested, or frustrated.

True connection with someone involves many non-verbal aspects. Vocal tone, posture, and facial expression are all types of nonverbal communication essential to creating a shared understanding with someone.

"Look at me!" A request such as this may come from a parent trying to gain a child's attention, or from a child climbing to the top of outdoor play equipment. Perhaps it comes from a spouse or partner looking down at a mobile phone during dinner. Eye contact is one form of nonverbal communication that makes a major difference in the way relationships develop and are maintained.[6]

But of all forms of human communication, nonverbal communication is probably the least understood and most confusing. In other words, nonverbals can easily be misunderstood. They are sloppy and even dangerous partly because they might not be truly reflective regarding what someone is thinking, feeling, or suggesting.

The numerous ways our messages can be misunderstood without face-to-face contact is mind boggling. Just think about the last time you texted the word "hey" and consider how it might have been taken. Over coffee, a student of mine named Shelly complained about the complex symbolism of a simple "hey" she received. "When my friend Joel texts me 'hey,'" she explained, "I've learned that it means he wants to get together. But when Frank texts the same word, he's just saying hello. When I get the same text from guys I meet on campus, it means they want to go on a date. It's frustrating."

Still, even nonverbal cues can help us communicate clearly, in tune with visual or aural words. For instance, a friend says something that might mean compliance or acquiescence to an idea, or flat-out agreement. But her face looks puzzled. We need to consider how looking puzzled fits with the person's words. By combining words and nonverbals we can minimize mixed messages.

A wife agrees to a husband's large expenditure for a motorcycle. She's smiling and may say "yes, that's fine." But what if her shoulders are slumped, and she's not making eye contact? Her husband needs to consider the possible mixed messages before running out to purchase the bike. Nonverbal cues provide important information. The key is paying attention to them.

American philosopher and author Dallas Willard wrote, "The first act of love is always the giving of attention."[7] Careful relationship communication involves attentive listening and close observation of the verbal and nonverbal messages in conversation. We learn much about one another by paying attention to the pauses and silences as well as the expressions, gestures, and body language that don't make use of words at all.

Silence is one such cue. It can mean a great deal or nothing much. We can grow relationships by learning how to read another's nonverbal cues. We learn over time what others mean even when they don't use clearly spoken or written language. Muddied language, both verbal and nonverbal, makes it much more challenging to stay on course with friendships, families, and workplaces that flourish with healthy communication. Philosopher Max

Picard wasn't responding to the clanging din of information and voices that affects us in the digital age, but he could've been when he said, "All things are present all the time in an atmosphere of noisy rebelliousness, and man, who has lost the silence in which to sink the all-too-many, all-too-present multitude of things, allows them to evaporate and vanish in the all-consuming emptiness of language."[8]

Communication Context

Other thinkers remind us that meanings are typically found in context that has developed over time. These meanings are interlaced in the entire elaborate system of culture and aren't easily or immediately untangled in a single conversation.

So when attempting to have thriving relationships, we always need to interpret another's words in context. The larger context for our relational communication is culture—that is, ways of life that include everything humans create and use, from toys and TV to architecture, rituals, values, and belief. Think of all of the different places we communicate including coffee shops, classrooms, kitchens, game rooms, libraries, workplaces, hair and nail salons, and many more. The rules about what can be said and how it can be said change for each one. What, when, why, and how to speak, gestures, motion, laughter, and so much more, depend on the communication context.

For example, Eric Brende, who researched the close ties of the Amish community for his doctoral dissertation, lived and worked with the Pennsylvania Amish for 12 months. He noted the ways in which relationships were built without words among this subculture that avoids most new technology. One of the ways he noted how relationships were built was in how important the lulls in the work day communicated a strong sense of authentic community and belonging:

> The work was heavy and the day long, yes. But there was something pleasantly haphazard about the scheduling; there were lulls. Lulls waiting between wagonloads. Lulls caused by lack of coordination of the persons overseeing, if anyone was overseeing. Lulls for eating and drinking. Lulls here, lulls there. . . . [T]hese gaps could easily have been overlooked. The lulls did not constitute mere empty time; conversation, for instance, often continued

unabated when the work stopped. Lulls were part of the natural flow of human activity and rhythm. They were a testimony to genuine human leisure.[9]

Even in our own lives, lulls can be lovely. These moments of silence, solitude, and casual conversations that build our friendships aren't as prevalent as they once were. In fact, the pace of life has so exponentially increased in the last 25 years that the notion of a lull is something of an anomaly. The expectation that we're always busy has become a badge some of us wear to let everyone around us know how important we are. Taking time to eat our dinners slowly with friends and family, staying afterwards to talk without an agenda are examples of lulls. Or we might use meetings in coffee shops as lulls from the everyday hustle and bustle. Silence and its friendly sister solitude can help break the pace and all-encompassing demands of our hurried culture.

Self-knowledge, Silence, and Solitude

Another sound of silence is spiritual formation. There is a silence beyond and within words that supports what's said and shapes it. Max Picard reminds us when he writes that "Speech rises from the bed of silence."[10] Thomas Merton connects reflective, prayerful silence with spiritual formation and our apprehension of faith:

> If there is not silence beyond and within the many words of doctrine, there is no religion, only a religious ideology. For religion goes beyond words and actions and attains the ultimate truth only in silence and love. Where this silence is lacking, where there are only the many words' and not the One Word, then there is much bustle and activity but no peace, no deep thought, no understanding, no inner quiet.[11]

We may know we're part of God's beloved intellectually, but spending time in quiet solitude and silence helps us remember it. As we turn away from the noise of everyday life, we open ourselves to know God beyond our intellect. We begin to feel God's love within our hearts. Spending time in solitude with God helps us remember that we belong to Him. We begin to understand the depth of His love in a new way. He who is Truth will lead us into all truth.[12]

The power of solitude and silence also work toward the good for others. Learning to listen to the voice of the Lord helps us listen to the person we love no matter how they may have disappointed us or squandered our love in the past. Awareness of the personhood of the lover or friend affects the way we communicate our love, yet it necessitates looking beyond the masks and external distractions that keep us at emotional and spiritual distances from one another. To start, it means getting in touch with one's own interior, an endeavor much supported by the regular practice of solitude. Silence is a key part of learning to communicate well with those we love. In silence we're confronted by our thoughts and estimation of who the other is and have an opportunity to embrace the reality of others instead of striving to grasp a false idea of who they are. There is a strong connection between the self-knowledge discovered in the quiet places of solitude and one's ability to give love and receive love. Once again, Merton helps us perceive this connection with wider, societal implications:

> When society is made up of men who know no interior solitude it can no longer be held together by love: and consequently, it's held together by a violent and abusive authority. But when men are violently deprived of the solitude and freedom which are their due, the society in which they live becomes putrid; it festers with servility, resentment, and hate. No amount of technological progress will cure the hatred that eats away the vitality of materialistic society like a spiritual cancer. The only cure is, and must always be, spiritual.[13]

Conclusion

The bravery one needs to embark on a truly relational life starts with tender notes of silence coming from quiet confidence and comfort with who we are on the inside, and acceptance of others. The only one who can truly give this to us is God. This requires regular practice of silence and solitude and it takes time. Silence provides fertile ground in which the roots of relationship become established and may eventually blossom into deep and lasting love.

But silence is only one of the powerful nonverbal communication cues that help us understand ourselves and others. In this chapter, I've explored several ways our nonverbal cues can be powerful tools to help us cultivate thriving friendships and families that continue to grow in closeness and love. I've emphasized silence, perhaps because it has made such a difference in my own relationships. Silence and solitude nurture our life with God in the Spirit, and ultimately work toward the good, the noble, and the pure in all of our relationships. To go further, I'll take the last chapter of this book to discuss the truth about prayer.

Questions for Reflection

1. How might we use the gift of silence as a part of our communication toolkit?

2. Is there a silence that's harmful to relationships? If so, what is it and why is it so tempting to revert to it when conflict arises? Think of a personal example and write it out.

3. Among your primary relationships, think of one that could use a regular rhythm of silence. Why do you think this is so, and how might you go about using silence as a gift?

Chapter 12

Powering Relationships with Prayer

Pray without ceasing, give thanks in all circumstances; for this is the will of God in Christ Jesus for you.
— 1 Thessalonians 5:17–18, ESV

THERE ONCE was this girl I knew who understood the path to successful employment. She knew it involved taking the initiative not only to apply for a good job, but also to follow up several times. This would ensure a potential employer of the worthiness of the future employee. In a slow economy when no one was getting hired, this 20-something woman thought she knew how to go about it. And she was right. The problem was that her husband was content to be passive about the process and truly thought the job would simply fall into his hands out of heaven. This, as you might imagine, for my friend, was a serious problem that caused every kind of conflict in their young marriage. Both were earnest Christians. Both trusted God to provide. But it wasn't until my friend really started praying for her husband that things began to change. There is a positive ending to this story, but it's rather beside my point. Ultimately, my friend prayed for her husband and talked to the Lord about him instead of continuing to talk to him about it. An interesting thing happened. First, her heart toward him expanded. Next, their affection for each other increased and their love seemed to deepen. Finally, he landed a decent job, but it took a while.

In this last chapter, I'll take some time to explore the multi-faceted power of prayer, particularly some of the ways prayer can strengthen our closest relationships. Then, revisiting the importance of listening and openness, conversation and conflict resolution, affection and intimacy, I'll talk about the ways these elements of relationship come together. Of everything that's important in the cultivation of healthy relationships, I've left prayer last in hopes that it will remain foremost on the minds of my readers.

Prayer Changes Things

When I was a young girl, I often saw this phrase on bumper stickers. A bit like today's memes, the cars in front of me displayed a truth that I had yet to discover—prayer changes things! What I found out as I walked through those early years in faith is that an amazing thing happens when you begin to pray. It's not just that one or two changes appear in your week. Prayer changes everything.

Prayer isn't about doing. It's not about obtaining results. That doesn't mean we stop asking God for something specific. Scripture teaches us to bring everything, by prayer and petition, with thanksgiving, to God.[1] Prayer is about communion. It isn't a means to an end. Prayer is an expression of love and dependence on God. It's an act of declaration, reminding us that we need His presence and providence. It's a holy fellowship.

When we pray for someone, we bring them into that circle of fellowship with God. Praying for the ones we love helps us stay attentive to the actions and attitudes that keep these relationships strong. Prayer helps us remain constant in devotion to God and those we love. Like my friend with the husband who took no initiative to get a job, there are times when the best thing to do is to pray. Praying for the friend, spouse, parent, child, or sibling does much to turn relational problems around. There are several reasons for this.

Prayer Is Practical

When we start praying for someone it stirs compassion rather than judgment. Instead of criticizing or judging those we love, when we pray for them, our hearts can't help but be touched by the Father's love and the relationship stands a much better chance of being strengthened instead of torn apart. The change of heart doesn't usually happen instantly but can take some time. Like my friend who was frustrated about her husband's lack of motivation to find a job, her heart was changed through the process of prayer.

Although things might look worse before they look better, praying for a stubborn spouse instead of chastising him will help evoke a tender attitude, one that's fertile ground for the seeds of love to germinate and blossom. It's difficult to pray for another and not grow in compassion and love toward them, especially if you're convinced that you're right.

When we start praying for someone, it helps us keep from trying to fix them. Praying for the one we care about takes the responsibility and results out of our hands and puts it directly at the feet of the Lord. Jesus was clear when He said He would bear our burdens: "Come to me all who are weary and burdened, and I will give you rest" (Matt. 11:28–30, NIV).

Time spent praying for those we love fosters patience and other fruit in our own lives. We can move from being an impatient person to a patient one as the fruit of the Spirit begins to blossom in our lives.[2] Patience is but one fruit that begins to appear in our lives as we're transformed by Christ. As Paul told the Romans, "Be transformed by the renewal of your minds, no longer conformed to the ways of this world" (Rom. 12:2, NIV).

Another part of the transformation involves keeping our ego in the right place. Many, if not most, of us struggle with being humble. Prayer helps drive away that natural born arrogance, bringing humility into our hearts and helping us to remember that we're not the center of the universe. When we begin praying for others, it's not that those prayers are always answered in the way we expect. But a funny thing happens on the way to the altar of worship. We learn surrender. We learn sacrifice. We learn to let God be in the driver's seat of our lives. Indeed, prayer changes us.

The busyness and pace of life in our digital culture makes it appear impractical and even impossible for some of us to slow down. But so much in life requires waiting, quieting our busy minds, and not rushing ahead. Waiting is counterintuitive, but it doesn't mean we do nothing. The posture of waiting in prayer involves expectancy, the type of waiting that's pregnant with trust and belief that the Lord will do that which He has said he will do. Such waiting on the Lord renews our strength.[3] Like Simeon who watched with expectancy while he waited for God to send the promised Messiah, we build spiritual muscle as we "watch and wait" for our relationships to blossom into greater fullness (Luke 2:25–35, NIV). Waiting on the Lord in prayer may look different when praying with someone else, but it involves the same watching and waiting together for the Lord to provide guidance, comfort, or direction. This is a type of prayer that sounds passive, but it's active, alive with expectancy. It's something I've come to think of as active passivity.

One of the biggest lessons I learned about patience in prayer is the ongoing adjustments to my own attitudes and behaviors. Watching and waiting makes room for much reflection. It's humbling to wait, but waiting allows us room to see our own imperfections and lack of ability to effectuate necessary change. A heart that's been humbled in recognition of its own imperfections will begin to use words more wisely and will speak with grace and give the others the benefit of the doubt. Watching and waiting in this often helpless state gives us inspiration to forgive others' imperfections and mistakes. Communication professor Paul Soukup brings insight to the way in which the salve of God's love and the act of forgiveness can offer healing to relationships. He explains that restorative communication is like a

> sacred trust, motivated not by the power of one partner to dominate the other, not by the desire to monopolize the conversation, but by the desire to let conversational partners speak what most concerns them. In this communication, we open the door for another by humbling ourselves.[4]

Humility is perhaps the most underrated element of love. It's the part that's 100% necessary if we want to keep our relationships flourishing. Without humility, conflict seems to multiply. Without humility we too easily allow simple misunderstandings and normal human weaknesses to undermine even the strongest of relationships. Prayer helps us walk in humility and understand that, ultimately, we're not the ones in control.

Besides being counterintuitive, prayer is also counter-cultural. When everything around us screams "now!", it's definitively countercultural to wait and pray. Our propensity to run ahead and do whatever it takes to make something happen is part of our human nature. But jumping into action without the peace of God often makes more of a mess of things. Jesus's example is to watch and pray. In fact, the scriptures tell us that Jesus only did what He heard the Father tell Him to do.[5] That's a tall order for us, but knowing that He promises to direct and guide us evokes a sense of hope and grows us in trusting our Lord to lead the way.

Stability to Ability

Being grounded in prayer brings a deeper level of stability to our lives which aids our ability to maintain strong, life-giving relationships. Prayer helps keep doubt at bay and renews the hope that's found in Christ, providing residual positive effects in every area of life. French theologian and philosopher Jacques Ellul speaks to the need for prayer and its place in the life of a believer. He acknowledges our tendency to resist prayer:

[W]e shall have to conquer ourselves in the face of that gnawing doubt, the continual question, 'what's the use?' It is not merely a matter of wanting to pray, but of praying a genuine prayer. On that score we are caught up in a struggle against the life direction given by our consumer society, which neither knows nor is able to suggest as the meaning of our work, the joy of our life and the value of our society as anything other than a higher level of consumption.[6]

Although we may grow weary of praying when prayers seem to go unanswered, it's important to press through and continue to pray because our communion with God is the very ground of our strength.

Prayer as Communion: With-ness

Prayer isn't just about getting answers or seeing change. Nor is it confined to the formal liturgies taught in our churches. Prayer helps us remember we have a heavenly Father who loves us, knows that we need Him, and is ready to guide and comfort. It's also about getting through the waiting. We wait for the healing; we wait for the answer; we wait for a positive turnaround in our finances, housing, and relationships. Praying for others is a way to stay mindful in the relationship as well as a reminder that God is a part of the relationship.

We don't always realize that God is invested in our lives. He didn't just create us and leave. He is with us. He cares about our friendships, our longings, our marriages, our wider families, and our world. Let's never forget that God created us to commune with Him. I referenced this earlier; it's something I've come to call "with-ness." With-ness allows us to walk in the way of intimate awareness of God's presence. It's the prayer of communion with Him, the prayer of intimacy in which we fellowship with the Lord throughout the day. Ellul suggests that this type of prayer is linked with joy and true freedom. Accordingly, prayer

is the impugning of my anguish, of my pessimism, through joy. It is the bursting of my bonds through freedom. It does all that without giving me even the shadow of a good conscience, for in prayer I know very well (and through direct experience with that without which there is no prayer) that this joy, this freedom, and this hope do not come from me.[7]

As we fellowship with Him, the contentment, joy, peace, and every other good that's associated with the very best of our relationships begins to bear fruit.

Maintaining a healthy habit of prayer reminds us of who and whose we are. It establishes a strong foundation, grounding our identity in Christ rather than the fleeting trends of popular culture. Prayer helps us recognize and establish our identity as a child of God. The wise words of Catholic priest and author Henri Nouwen remind us that "praying means giving up a false security, no longer looking for arguments which will protect you if you get pushed into a corner."[8] The idea of "letting go and letting God" is pertinent here. It's closely connected to exchanging the desire to control things for a deeper trust in God. Through prayer as communion with God we learn to build our lives on a foundation that's solid. As the "house of relationship" is built, our relationships are built on that sturdy foundation.

Prayer and Digital Domination

Learning to live in faith instead of false expectations and fantastical illusions of love may take a lifetime. But developing the habit of prayer—perhaps one of the most counterintuitive practices in our busy world—gives us a solid place to start. Prayer and faith go hand-in-hand, but the two aren't synonymous; rather, prayer flows from faith and faith deepens through prayer. Prayer doesn't create faith but puts us in the right posture for our faith to grow. Ellul explains that "prayer is not a work of faith. It's a possibility of the work of faith. That's why Scripture teaches us to pray without ceasing, for faith is completely sterile without this respiration."[9]

As we pray it reminds us of the commitments we've made to love, care for, and cherish others. An intentional daily time with the Lord gives us a place to take the doubt that sometimes plagues us.[10] Without it we're easily pulled away by the many distractions in our busy technological society. The regular practice of prayer helps us to stay close to God. Through prayer we can discover a deeper place of communion—a place of intimacy in our relationship with God, one that's steady, strong, filled with peace, content with His purposes, and overflowing with relationships that thrive and grow deeper with each passing year.

A heart that has been humbled in recognition of its own imperfections will begin to use words more wisely and will take care to speak with grace and give the other the benefit of the doubt. In this way, we stay open and willing to forgive others' imperfections and mistakes.

Praying for and with One Another

Praying together is a practice that creates an emotional intimacy or closeness that comes from holding each other's needs and concerns up to the Lord. The important point isn't so much the number of hours we spend praying for others, but that we do it in the first place. One of the ways this became a strength in my own marriage was when my husband and I were in our twenties. It was in the busyness of raising three children that he and I realized our daily responsibilities were crowding out the very things that brought us together. So right there, at the height of our busyness, we made a choice to get up at least fifteen minutes before the little ones rose and take the first five or ten minutes to say hello, talk about the previous day, and open the day with a prayer. Five minutes turned into fifteen, and in six months' time we got up 45 minutes earlier and loved every minute of it.

Morning coffee time with my husband has made a space for listening, openness, and face-to-face conversation, elements of communication that are so vital for keeping a relationship healthy and strong. It continues today. We talk about our schedules, share our concerns, and hear about each other's activities from the day before. Sometimes one of us brings a thought about the Lord or a Scripture we've been pondering, and we sit quietly together and mediate on it. Other times we pray very intentionally together, seeking direction for ourselves or specific people. A few minutes first thing in the morning is a great way to start the day and affirm the oneness we share. It's also a good place to confess to one another the ways each may have fallen short the day before. Without the daily touchpoint it's so easy to drift away from each other.

This issue isn't new. Drifting from an active, living faith isn't something that emerged in recent history. Despite the massive distractions we face online, the tendency to forget God did not begin with the digital age. Quaker mystic Thomas Kelly addressed this drift in his short yet powerful book, *A Testament of Devotion*, when he explained:

> Our real problem in failing to center down is not a lack of time,
> it is, I fear, in too many of us, lack of joyful enthusiastic delight
> in Him, lack of deep-drawing love directed toward Him at every

hour of the day and night. I think it is clear that I am talking about a revolutionary way of living. Religion isn't something to be added to our other duties, and thus makes our lives yet more complex. The life with God is the center of life, and all else is remodeled and integrated by it. It gives the singleness of eye.[11]

Kelly's notion of "singleness of eye" suggests that we allow the love of God to be the lens through which we see. How does this happen without prayer? It doesn't. Yet, when we devote ourselves to prayer, rather than attempting to ground our relationships in natural love, Christ becomes our grounding. Christ-as-center offers supernatural supply. His love enlarges our hearts and helps us grow in capacity to offer love to others in grace and in truth. The practice of prayer draws us into a place of being where communion with God is as natural as breathing. Prayer refreshes, fulfills, and expands our lives.

Prayer may also be the truest antidote to loneliness. Even though people need people, knowing the Lord is present can stem the loneliness we feel when no one else is around. The loneliness epidemic in the country has been well-established and documented in recent years.[12] It's so important to reach out to those we love and stay closely connected. In the same way, taking regular time in prayerful communion with the Lord can keep the loneliness from turning into despair. Such times of quiet and solitude have the potential to renew and revive our weary souls.

Love is the most precious gift we can give one another and it's worth the effort to press through whatever struggle presents itself. It's far too easy in our hurried culture to brush past the ones we love with hardly a word, let alone a hug, kiss, or kind word. This doesn't have to be so. Pausing for a kind word or caring gesture may be countercultural, but so is the Gospel of Jesus Christ. His words and life point us to a kingdom that isn't of this world but an eternal one that's opposite of this world in every way.

The Power of Prayer in the Flame of Fire

Throughout my life I've experienced the power of prayer. When I was a child, a roaring fire started in a field on the farm where I grew up. My father rushed into the house and told my mother to get all the children (five of us) and leave. My grandmother, who lived with us, went into her bedroom, got down on her knees and prayed. The fire miraculously went out. Another time my father was in a tragic accident. The doctors said he would never walk again. We prayed. Within six months he was walking. My father didn't have a relationship with Jesus Christ. We prayed, and even though the answer didn't come for many years, eventually he came to know Christ personally. I didn't marry until I was 44. I prayed for a child. I thought I'd waited too long. But when I was forty-seven the Lord answered my prayer and gave us a son.

Our living, loving, eternal God is a God who listens, who talks with us, and who answers our prayers. Sometimes life hands us something very difficult like when I lost a loved one. I know that in our darkest hours we can turn to the God of all comfort. We can go to Him at any time, day, or night, and He hears. In the quietness of our inner life, we can commune with our loving Father. God can't only heal our bodies, but he can also heal our emotions. When relationships go awry, God can help us to forgive and to love. As you think about your life and your relationship with the Lord, are you enjoying open honest communication with Him?

— **Geraldine E. Forsberg**, Senior Instructor,
Western Washington University

Conclusion

As we come to the end of this final chapter, we've looked at several aspects of prayer and explored some of the ways prayer can enrich our lives. Prayer is a part of our worship. It grounds us and helps us grow deeper in our relationship with God and others. It's part of the way we build our "house of relationship." Dwelling there is what gives us the inspiration and fortitude to press through the most difficult and even tragic moments in life. Unfortunately, we too often choose ourselves over the ones we love, causing the roof of our house to deteriorate or collapse altogether. Our prayers are the pillars that will hold it up. Fidelity to the practice of prayer is key to our ability to find solace and direction when we're away from our dear friends or family. It's not that our prayers in a time of need have no bearing but, rather, that strength and consolation arise from an ongoing, steady practice of prayer.

In closing, it's of immeasurable worth to remember to walk with an attitude of humility. Understanding we're not exempt from being offensive, nor are we pleasing at all times to those we love. Even in the best of situations we'll fail each other sometimes, but God's perfect love isn't beyond our reach. As we give ourselves more readily and steadily to Him in prayer, His love echoes throughout our lives and transcends the natural order—it's supernatural. As trust builds and our human relationships are strengthened, the emotional space necessary to continue to flourish expands, but the potential for misunderstandings and the regular need to practice forgiveness is ever present.

Sometimes I perceive relationships as a rugged landscape, like a wilderness. I see relationships as an untamed land where we walk side by side, exploring the nuance of each other's personalities and ideas. The landscape of relationships is the landscape of love. Discerning the way forward means stopping regularly to observe our surroundings and remain attentive to any changes. It means discussing what we've gained from our travels and finding time for fun and refreshment. Finding the rhythm in that walk together is a lifelong process.

Whether we're in a relationship with a lifelong partner, a best friend, family members, or a close community of faith, learning to walk in the rhythm of love's terrain can at times be agonizing, but is also the most rewarding part of life. Slowing down to enjoy the journey and making the most of our time with those we cherish will need to be increasingly intentional as our digital media becomes even more pervasive and embedded in our daily habits. Taking the needed measures to let love, instead of technology, lead us is key to moving our relationships from something we manage on the run to a place we dwell in, deeply.

Paying attention to the holy habits of love creates a deposit of patience, compassion, wisdom, and light. This is the light of the Lord. It's more than a candle in the window or something we hope for at the end of a tunnel. The light of the Lord beams its holy presence. The Father of lights gives us the opportunity to walk in His presence and helps us to walk in greater fullness of His love each day. He is the Light of the world and darkness won't overtake it![13]

Questions for Reflection

1. Is prayer practical? Explain your answer.

2. How do you connect the power of prayer with the ability to love your friends and family through times of disagreement or anger?

3. Take at least five minutes each day in the coming week to write your prayers for at least one person you love. Return to this practice each day for one week and then describe what changes (if any) you are seeing in your feelings toward them.

Notes

Chapter 1
Understand the Pitfalls of Mediated Multitasking

[1] Jeff Olson, "How Multitasking Hurts Your Relationships," *Mayo Clinic*, July 11, 2016, https://newsnetwork.mayoclinic.org/discussion/mayo-clinic-minute-how-multitasking-hurts-your-relationships/.

[2] Neil Postman, "Five Things We Need to Know About Technological Change" (speech, Denver, CO, March 28, 1998).

[3] Postman, "Five Things."

[4] Patrick Van Kessel, "How Americans feel about the satisfactions and stresses of modern life," *Pew Research Center*, February 5, 2020, https://www.pewresearch.org/short-reads/2020/02/05/how-americans-feel-about-the-satisfactions-and-stresses-of-modern-life/.

[5] For the ten years between 2008 and 2018, reportage of generalized anxiety disorder rose exponentially. Throughout the two-year duration of the global pandemic, the figure rose over 50%. The most was in young adults (ages 18–24). Among other sources, these figures were reported in the National Library of Medicine. Lisa Damour, "New Study Links Phone Use and Mental Health in Teens," *CBS News*, video interview, July 3, 2017, 0:45, https://www.youtube.com/watch?v=HjJ4tnePhbw.

[6] Julian Roberts-Grmela, "Emotional Stress Remains a Top Challenge to Keeping Students Enrolled," The Chronicle of Higher Education, March 23, 2023, https://www.chronicle.com/article/emotional-stress-remains-a-top-challenge-to-keeping-students-enrolled.

[7] See Damour, "New Study Links Phone Use and Mental Healthy in Teens."

[8] Emma Kauana Osorio and Emily Hyde, "The Rise of Anxiety and Depression Among Young Adults in the United States," *Ballard Brief*, Winter 2021, https://ballardbrief.byu.edu/issue-briefs/the-rise-of-anxiety-and-depression-among-young-adults-in-the-united-states.

[9] Kory Floyd, *Communicating Affection* (Cambridge: Cambridge University Press, 2009), 8, https://www.cambridge.org/core/books/communicating-affection/5091019BB8095631083C781FDF48E2C5.

[10] Continuous Partial Attention (CPA) is a phrase coined by Linda Stone in 1997. It suggests communication behavior that's "always-on" scanning, scrolling, seeking to know and be known. It has become increasingly common to live this way in the Internet generation. For further reading, see Harriet Griffey, "The Lost Art of Concentration: Being Distracted in a Digital World," *The Guardian*, October 12, 2018, https://www.theguardian.com/lifeandstyle/2018/oct/14/the-lost-art-of-concentration-being-distracted-in-a-digital-world.

[11] Gregory Reynolds, "Interview with Gregory Reynolds," interview by Ken Myers, *Mars Hill Audio Journal* 90, 2008 (February 23, 2024) https://marshillaudio.org/products/mh-90-m.

[12] Kenneth Gergen, *The Saturated Self: Dilemmas of Identity in Contemporary Life* (New York: Perseus Books, 1991).

[13] Aleks Krotowski, "Robin Dunbar: We can only ever have 150 friends at most…", *The Guardian*, March 13, 2010, https://www.theguardian.com/technology/2010/mar/14/my-bright-idea-robin-dunbar.

[14] Neil Postman, *Amusing Ourselves to Death* (New York: Penguin, 2010).

[15] Dan Allender, "Trauma and the Body," *Allender Center at the Seattle School*, https://theallendercenter.org/2016/09/trauma-and-the-body/.

[16] Gergen, *The Saturated Self*, 175.

[17] Gergen, *The Saturated Self*, 175.

[18] Monica Anderson, Michelle Faverio, and Eugenie Park, "How Teens and Parents Approach Screen Time," *Pew Research Center*, March 11, 2024, https://www.pewresearch.org/internet/2024/03/11/how-teens-and-parents-approach-screen-time/.

[19] Vaishnavi S. Nakshine, Preeti Thute, Mahalaqua Nazli Khatib, and Bratati Sarkar, "Increased Screen Time as a Cause of Declining Physical, Psychological Health, and Sleep Patterns: A Literary Review," *Cureus* 14, no. 10 (October 2022), https://doi.org/10.7759/cureus.30051.

[20] "The Real Strength of Weak Ties," *Stanford News*, September 15, 2022, https://news.stanford.edu/2022/09/15/real-strength-weak-ties/.

[21] "The Real Strength." The 2022 Sanford University study points to the strength of weak ties theory as a means of social satisfaction. Without the numerous small snatches of conversation that occur throughout the day, the sense of belonging to a community suffers.

[22] The ongoing research and reportage of U.S. Surgeon General, Vivek Murthy, strongly suggests a correlation between social media and the epidemic of loneliness, particularly in the absence of physical presence. Earlier research done by Sherry Turkle points to the same findings. Her book, *Reclaiming Conversation* is an excellent read. Sherry Turkle, *Reclaiming Conversation: The Power of Talk in a Digital Age* (New York: Penguin, 2015), 26.

Chapter 2
Feeling the Power of Presence

[1] Kory Floyd, *Communicating Affection: Interpersonal Behavior and Social Context* (New York: Cambridge University Press, 2006), 95.

[2] Walter J. Ong, *The Presence of the Word* (Minneapolis: University of Minnesota Press, 1967), 130.

[3] Turkle's research with 5th, 6th, and 7th graders is eye-opening. The willingness of children to admit their loneliness is startling. For details, see: Sherry Turkle, *Reclaiming Conversation: The Power of Talk in a Digital Age* (New York: Penguin, 2015).

[4] Wayne Altree, *Why Talk? A Conversation about Language with Walter J. Ong* (San Francisco: Chandler and Sharp Publishers, 1973), 15.

[5] Ong, *The Presence of the Word*, 125.

[6] Brother Lawrence, *The Practice of the Presence of God* (Springdale, PA: Whitaker House, 1982).

[7] Martin Buber, *I and Thou* (Princeton, NJ: Princeton University Press, 1949).

[8] Buber, *I and Thou*, 44.

[9] Thomas Merton, "Love and Need: Is Love a Package or a Message?" in *The Reach of Dialogue*, eds. Robert Anderson, Kenneth Cissna, and Ronald C. Arnett (Cresskill, NJ: Hampton, 1994), 251.

[10] Wendell Berry, *Life Is a Miracle: An Essay Against Modern Superstition* (Washington, DC: Counterpoint, 2001), 55.

[11] Of the multiple reasons for the importance of spending time in each other's presence is facial primacy. Neuroscientist Antonio Damasio conducted many experiments on people's reactions to the human face. Dr. Damasio conducted a study involving a large set of neutral-expression faces—both male and female—in which participants were asked to rank each face according to how trustworthy it appeared. People's faces were divided into five categories. Some inspired extreme trust, others evoked fear. Ultimately, the study revealed a strong connection between trust and facial expression. For more details, see Damasio's interview with Paul Raeburn: Antonio Damasio, interview by Paul Raeburn, *Talk of the Nation*, NPR, July 24, 2009, https://www.npr.org/2009/07/24/106974470/how-does-the-brain-decide-who-to-trust.

[12] Sherry Turkle, *Alone Together: Why We Expect More from Technology and Less from Each Other* (New York: Basic Books, 2011), 293.

[13] Justin K. R. Collom, "Lost in Automation: How Technology's Dark Side is Ruining Customer Service," *LinkedIn*, May 6, 2023, https://www.linkedin.com/pulse/lost-automation-how-technologys-dark-side-ruining-customer-collom.

[14] Mollie Rube, Morgan Stosic, Jessica Correal, and Danielle Blanch-Hartigan, (ed. Nora Dunbar), "Is Technology Enhancing or Hindering Interpersonal Communication? A Framework and Preliminary Results to Examine the Relationship Between Technology Use and Nonverbal Decoding Skill," *Frontiers in Psychology* 11, (January 2020): https://doi.org/10.3389/fpsyg.2020.611670.

[15] This triangulated study involved survey, interviews, focus groups, and written response to the questions: "What did you do with the silence you experienced during the 24-hour span without electronic/digital media? And, "What emotions did you feel as a result of this experiment, both during the exercise and afterward?"

[16] T. S. Eliot, "Choruses from 'The Rock,'" in *Collected Poems*, 1909–1935, ed. Jewell Spears Brooker (Published online March 2010. Cambridge University Press, 1936), 179, https://www.cambridge.org/core/books/abs/t-s-eliot/collected-poems-19091935-1936/8E8359FF27B852ADD0534A30B4EDBB87.

Chapter 3
Avoiding Relational Fantasies

[1] This was an American sitcom TV series that aired on NBC from 1965–1970. Barbara Eden played the role of a genie in a bottle. When Larry Hagman (filling the role of U.S. astronaut Tony Nelson) rescued her from the bottle he found on the beach, suddenly she was free from her 2,000-year captivity and his wish was her command.

[2] A nimbus 2000 is a vibrating broomstick, used in the Harry Potter series as part of his magical toolkit. It's part of the fantasy book series written by United Kingdom author J. K. Rowling in 1997, and published by Bloomsbury in the United States.

[3] Gallop reports that although positive emotions show signs of improvement, the negative experience index continues to remain high. Julie Ray, "Global Rise in Unhappiness Stalls," *Gallup*, June 27, 2023, https://news.gallup.com/poll/507725/global-rise-unhappiness-stalls.aspx#:~:text=Worry%2C%20stress%20and%20sadness%20remained,second%20year%20in%20a%20row.

[4] Mayo Clinic Staff, "COVID-19 and your mental health," *Mayo Clinic*, April 4, 2024, https://www.mayoclinic.org/diseases-conditions/coronavirus/in-depth/mental-

health-covid-19/art-20482731#:~:text=Worldwide%20surveys%20done%20in%20 2020,still%20higher%20than%20before%202020.

[5] Charlie Warzel, "The Dark Side of Frictionless Technology: Living in an exhausting world of obsolescence," *The Atlantic Monthly Group*, September 20, 2022, https://www.theatlantic.com/newsletters/archive/2022/09/personal-tech-obsolete-user-experience/676838/.

[6] Quentin J. Schultze, *Communicating for Life: Christian Stewardship in Community and Media* (Grand Rapids, MI: Baker, 2000), 60.

[7] Dan Allender, interview by Rachael Clinton Chen, *The Allender Center*, May 28, 2022, https://theallendercenter.org/2022/05/why-story/.

[8] Justin R. Garcia, "Sexual Hookup Culture: A Review," *Review of General Psychology* 16, no. 2 (2012): 161–176, https://www.apa.org/monitor/2013/02/sexual-hookup-culture.pdf.

[9] Justin R. Garcia, Chris Reiber, Sean G. Massey, and Ann M. Merriwether, "Sexual Hook-Up Culture," *Monitor on Psychology* 44, no. 2 (February 2013), https://www.apa.org/monitor/2013/02/ce-corner.

[10] Lauren F. E. Galloway, "Does Movie Viewing Cultivate Unrealistic Expectations about Love and Marriage?" Master's Thesis (University Libraries, University of Nevada, Las Vegas, 2013).

[11] "The themes of books, plots of movies and television shows, and lyrics of numerous songs all demonstrate a permissive sexuality among consumers. The media suggests that uncommitted sex, or hookups, can be both physically and emotionally enjoyable and occur without 'strings.'" In: Justin R. Garcia, Chris Reiber, Sean G. Massey, and Ann M. Merriwether, "Sexual Hook-Up Culture," *Monitor on Psychology* 44, no. 2 (February 2013), https://www.apa.org/monitor/2013/02/ce-corner.

[12] 1 Corinthians 13:1–4 bears repeating: "If I speak in the tongues of men and of angels, but do not have love, I am only a resounding gong or a clanging cymbal. If I have the gift of prophecy and can fathom all mysteries and all knowledge, and if I have a faith that can move mountains, but do not have love, I am nothing. Love is patient and kind. It does not envy, it does not boast, it is not proud" (NIV). The Old Testament is full of references to true love and compassion. Deuteronomy 10:18 is one passage: "He defends the cause of the fatherless and the widow, and loves the foreigner residing among you, giving them food and clothing" (NIV). Love is taking care of widows and prisoners.

Chapter 4
Listening to Love

[1] Paul A. Soukup, *Out of Eden* (Boston: Pauline Books, 2007), 19.

[2] Barna Group, "What Non-Christians Want from Faith Conversations," *Barna*, February 19, 2019, https://www.barna.com/research/non-christians-faith-conversations/.

[3] Pedro Arrupe, SJ, "Teach Me Thy Ways," *Ignatian Spirituality*, A Service of Loyola Press, https://www.ignatianspirituality.com/ignatian-prayer/prayers-by-st-ignatius-and-others/teach-me-your-ways/.

[4] Janna Anderson, Lee Rainie, and Emily A. Vogels, "Experts Say the 'New Normal' in 2025 Will Be Far More Tech-Driven, Presenting More Big Challenges," *Pew Research Center*, February 18, 2021, https://www.pewresearch.org/internet/2021/02/18/experts-say-the-new-normal-in-2025-will-be-far-more-tech-driven-presenting-more-big-challenges/.

[5] Vivek Murthy, "How Music Heals Us, with Yo-Yo Ma," *U.S. Department of Health and Human Services*, YouTube video, 42:14, posted October 31, 2023, no longer available at https://www.youtube.com/watch?v=2dwkFOnM0rw. For more details on the U.S. Surgeon General's 82-page report in May of 2023, see: Vivek Murthy, *Our Epidemic of Loneliness and Isolation* (U.S. Department of Health and Human Services, Washington, DC. 2023), https://www.hhs.gov/sites/default/files/surgeon-general-social-connection-advisory.pdf.

[6] Jeremy Nobel, "Does Social Media Make You Lonely?," *Harvard Health Blog*, December 21, 2018, https://www.health.harvard.edu/blog/is-a-steady-diet-of-social-media-unhealthy-2018122115600.

[7] Tim Newman, "Anxiety in the West: Is It on the Rise?" *Medical News Today*, September 5, 2018, https://www.medicalnewstoday.com/articles/322877.

[8] Justin Rosenstein, one of the team members behind the 2010 addition of the "like button" on Facebook's social media platform reports that it was first dubbed the "awesome" button. It was intended to make the platform more fun, but because of it scrolling through Facebook became addictive. For more detail, see: Casey Newton, "The person behind the Like button says software is wasting our time," *The Verge*, March 25, 2018, https://www.theverge.com/2018/3/28/17172404/justin-rosenstein-asana-social-media-facebook-timeline-gantt.

[9] Nobel, "Does Social Media Make You Lonely?"

[10] A recent study found that loneliness affected the well-being and overall physical health of 46% of people surveyed throughout the United States. The reasons, however, appear to be mixed. Loneliness was described as a daily sense of being overwhelmed by isolation and growing social anxiety, and the dynamics factoring into these numbers on loneliness are diverse but often include the heavy use of social media. One study, for example, was conducted in 2018 by University of Pennsylvania researchers and reported a correlation between excessive Internet and social media use. These numbers were calculated prior to the global pandemic of 2020. Another study, published in 2022 found the same. For further investigation see: Hilde Thygesen, Tore Bonsaksen, Mariyana Schoultz, Mary Ruffolo, Janni Leung, Daicia Price, and Amy Østertun Geirdal, "Social Media Use and Its Associations With Mental Health 9 Months After the COVID-19 Outbreak: A Cross-National Study," *Frontiers in Public Health* 9 (January 2022), https://doi.org/10.3389/fpubh.2021.752004.

[11] Alexa Lardieri, "Study: Many Americans Report Feeling Lonely, Younger Generations More So," *U.S. News and World Report*, May 1, 2018, https://www.usnews.com/news/health-care-news/articles/2018-05-01/study-many-americans-report-feeling-lonely-younger-generations-more-so.

[12] Lardieri, "Many Americans Report."

[13] Rebeca A. Marin, Amy Christiansen, and David C. Atkins., "Infidelity and Behavioral Couple Therapy: Relationship Outcomes Over 5 Years Following Therapy," *Couple and Family Psychology: Research and Practice* 3, no. 1 (2014): 1–12, https://doi.org/10.1037/cfp0000012.

[14] Those who are hearing impaired and proficient in American Sign Language may listen even more intently because they are so closely observing the nonverbal facial cues and other gestures while reading lips and responding with sign language. Those of us with perfect hearing may in fact be poorer listeners if our hearts aren't attuned and sensitive to what the other is trying to communicate.

[15] Ellen Rose, "Continuous Partial Attention: Reconsidering the Role of Online

Learning in the Age of Interruption," *Educational Technology* 50, no. 4 (July–August 2010): 41–46.

[16] David Runcorn, *A Center of Quiet: Hearing God When Life is Noisy* (Downers Grove, IL: InterVarsity, 1990), 100.

Chapter 5
Speaking Conversationally

[1] Zara Abrams of the American Psychological Association (APA) outlines many of the reasons people steer away from conversation. For further study, see her article published in the APA's online newsletter, Zara Abrams, "Conversations are essential to our well-being. Psychologists are exploring the science of why they're so powerful," *American Psychological Association* 54, no. 8 (November 2023): https://www.apa.org/monitor/2023/11/conversations-key-to-wellbeing.

[2] John Mirk, a minister, first said this. It stuck. See Stacy Steinberg, "Children Seen but not Heard," *University of Florida Levin College of Law*, no. 24–6 (2024), https://papers.ssrn.com/sol3/papers.cfm?abstract_id=4445565.

[3] Robert Putnam, *Bowling Alone* (New York: Simon and Schuster, 2000).

[4] Sherry Turkle, *Life on the Screen: Identity in the Age of the Internet* (New York: Simon & Schuster, 1995).

[5] Simon and Garfunkel, "I Am a Rock," track 5 on *Sounds of Silence*, recorded 1965, Columbia Records, vinyl.

[6] Jon Durham-Peters, *Speaking into the Air* (Chicago: University of Chicago Press, 1999), 30.

[7] Sherry Turkle, *Reclaiming Conversation: The Power of Talk in a Digital Age* (New York: Penguin, 2015), 26.

[8] The relational tension involved both internally and externally is an idea built upon in 2011 by communication scholar Leslie Baxter, whose initial work in Relational Dialectics Theory (RDT) posits the push-and-pull of relational needs such as openness/closeness (or revealing/concealing), which are part of the intensity and dynamics of all relationships. According to RDT, her idea that "discourses often compete with one another" is a foundational part of the way relationships develop and are maintained (Leslie Baxter, *Voicing Relationships: A Dialogic Perspective* [Thousand oaks, CA, Sage, 2011], 75).

[9] Neil Postman, *Crazy Talk, Stupid Talk* (New York: Delacorte, 1976), 8.

[10] Postman, *Crazy Talk*, 98.

[11] Laura Smit, *Loves Me, Loves Me Not: The Ethics of Unrequited Love* (Ada, MI: Baker Academic), 94.

[12] Julia Wood and Steve Duck, *Composing Relationships* (Belmont, CA: Thompson-Wadsworth, 2006), 8.

[13] Julia T. Wood, *Relational Communication: Continuity and Change in Personal Relationships*, 2nd ed. (Belmont, CA: Wadsworth Publishing Company, 2000), 191.

[14] For a worthy and careful exposition of this connection, see Quentin Schultze's *Communicating for Life: Christian Stewardship in Community and Media, Upd. & Exp.* (Pasco, WA: Integratio Press, 2024).

[15] Kathleen Norris, *Acedia and Me* (New York: Penguin Random House, 2010), 142.

[16] Parker Palmer, *To Know as we are Known* (San Francisco: HarperCollins, 1993), 8.

Chapter 6
Discovering Paths Toward Intimacy

[1] The full verses in 2 Corinthians 13:11–12 give us the context of this Scripture: "Finally, brothers and sisters, rejoice! Strive for full restoration, encourage one another, be of one mind, live in peace. And the God of love and peace will be with you. Greet one another with a holy kiss" (NIV).

[2] C. S. Lewis, *The Four Loves* (New York: Hartcourt, Brace, 1960), 50–66.

[3] Alice Klein, "Sexual Desire May Be Triggered by Gentle Touch Sensors in Your Skin," *New Scientist*, October 5, 2021, https://www.newscientist.com/article/2292115-sexual-desire-may-be-triggered-by-gentle-touch-sensors-in-your-skin/.

[4] Taylor Mallory Holland, "The Science of Touch," *Dignity Health*, April 28, 2018, https://www.dignityhealth.org/articles/facts-about-touch-how-human-contact-affects-your-health-and-relationships.

[5] Denny Kenaston, "A House That Stands in Persecution: Corrie and Betsie Ten Boom's Home Life," *Ephrata Ministries*, 2024, http://www.ephrataministries.org/remnant-2002-11-corrie-and-betsie-ten-booms-home-life.a5w.

[6] Adeline Dimond, "Living in the Non-Virtual 'Meat World' of Real Life," *Medium*, May 9, 2020, https://medium.com/assemblage/living-in-the-non-virtual-meat-world-of-real-life-80134ee7779f.

[7] Although this book isn't explicitly about physical love, it must be said here that daily, regular affection in a marriage is a definite precursor to sexual fulfillment and regularity among most couples.

[8] Lynda Law Harrison, David B. Buller, Jerold L. Hale, and Mark A. de Turck, "Physiologic and Behavioral Effects of Gentle Human Touch on Preterm Infants," *Research in Nursing & Health* 23, no. 6 (December 19, 2000): 435–46, https://doi.org/10.1002/1098-240X(200012)23:63.0.CO;2-P.

[9] A variety of interpretations have been made when studying this New Testament letter. Knowing first that it's a greeting provides context.

[10] Ruth Haly Barton, *Sacred Rhythms* (Westmont, IL: IVP *Formatio*, 2009), 81.

[11] Ronald Rolheiser, *The Holy Longing: The Search for a Christian Spirituality* (New York: Image, 2014), 194.

[12] Rolheiser, *The Holy Longing*, 202.

[13] Thomas Merton, *Love and Living* (San Francisco: Harper One, 2002), 105.

Chapter 7
Thinking About Who You Are

[1] Thomas Merton, *The Inner Experience* (New York: Harper Collins, 2004), 36.

[2] Dick Meyer, *Why We Hate Us* (New York: Crown, 2009), 66.

[3] "Personality," *American Psychological Association*, accessed July 11, 2024, https://www.apa.org/topics/personality.

[4] For example, we're fearfully and wonderfully made. For full verse, see Psalm 139:13–16 (NIV); Colossians 2:10 (BLB), "[A]nd you are complete in Him, he is the head of all principality and power"; and 1 Corinthians 6:19 (NLT): "Don't you realize that your body is the temple of the Holy Spirit, who lives in you and was given to you by God? You don't belong to yourself."

[5] Malachi 3:6 (NKJV): "I am the Lord, and I do not change."

[6] Robert McGee, *Search for Significance: Seeing Your True Worth Through God's Eyes* (Nashville: Thomas Nelson, 2003), 147–150.

⁷ John 14:25–27 (NIV): "But when He, the Spirit of Truth comes, He will guide you into all truth."

⁸ Romans 12:9–18 (NKJV): "Let love be without hypocrisy. Abhor what is evil. Cling to what is good. Be kindly affectionate to one another with brotherly love, in honor giving preference to one another; not lagging in diligence, fervent in spirit, serving the Lord; rejoicing in hope, patient in tribulation, continuing steadfastly in prayer; distributing to the needs of the saints, given to hospitality. Bless those who persecute you; bless and do not curse. Rejoice with those who rejoice, and weep with those who weep. Be of the same mind toward one another. Do not set your mind on high things but associate with the humble. Do not be wise in your own opinion. Repay no one evil for evil. Have regard for god things in the sight of all men. It is possible, as much as depends on you, live peaceably with all men."

⁹ Charles Taylor, *The Ethics of Authenticity* (Cambridge, MA: Harvard University Press, 2018), 14.

¹⁰ BetterHelp Editorial Team, "Understanding Codependency and Codependent Behavior," *BetterHelp*, June 10, 2024, https://www.betterhelp.com/advice/relations/co-dependency-what-it-is-how-to-recognize-it-and-how-to-change-it/.

¹¹ Taylor, *The Ethics of Authenticity*, 59.

¹² Taylor, *The Ethics of Authenticity*, 10.

¹³ Recent warnings that connect the use of social media with child development and mental health have emerged from the U.S. Surgeon General's office. Dr. Vivek Murthy's research revealed the emotional, mental, and physical dangers of social media for children and has called for emergency measures to be taken by parents and schools. In his May 2023 advisory, he recommended that parents immediately set limits on phone use and urged Congress to swiftly develop health and safety standards for technology platforms. Murthy, *Our Epidemic of Loneliness and Isolation* (U.S. Department of Health and Human Services, Washington D.C. 2023).

¹⁴ Parker Palmer, *To Know as We are Known* (San Francisco: HarperCollins, 1993), 50.

Chapter 8
Growing Closer Emotionally

¹ "Man by nature is a social animal." This quote is a paraphrase of Aristotle's original statement in *Politics*, where he more precisely states that "man is by nature a political animal." See Aristotle, *Politics*, trans. Carnes Lord (Chicago: University of Chicago Press, 1984), 1253a2, p. 4.

² The English word "passion" is a derivative of the Latin verb *patior* is *pati, passus sum*, which means to suffer and endure according to the Oxford Reference Dictionary. *Oxford Reference*, s. v. "Passion," accessed July 5, 2024, https://www.oxfordreference.com/display/10.1093/acref/9780190681166.001.0001/acref-9780190681166-e-237.

³ Curt Thompson, *The Deepest Place* (Grand Rapids, MI: Zondervan, 2023), 14.

⁴ Thomas Merton, *Love and Living* (San Francisco: Harper One, 2002), 100.

⁵ Kory Floyd, *Communicating Affection* (Cambridge, England: Cambridge University Press, 2009), 95.

⁶ Martin Buber, *I and Thou* (Princeton, NJ: Princeton University Press, 1949).

⁷ In a study co-authored by Rutgers assistant professor of sociology, Lei Lei, *Rutger's Today* research blog reports that playing video games and living longer with

their parents are two reasons both young men and young women are having less sex. For further reading, see: "Why are Young Adults Having Less Casual Sex?," *Rutgers*, March 22, 2021,https://www.rutgers.edu/news/why-are-young-adults-having-less-casual-sex.

[8] John Bowlby, *Attachment and Loss*, vol. 3, *Loss: Sadness and Depression* (New York: Basic Books, 1980).

[9] Henri Nouwen, *Lifesigns: Intimacy, Fecundity, and Ecstasy in Christian Perspective* (London: Image Books, 1989), 36.

[10] Matthew 13:16–17 (NIV) reports what happened at the time of Jesus's baptism. As the Spirit of God descended upon Jesus in the form of a dove, the Father's voice spoke, saying "this is my Son, whom I love, with him I am well-pleased."

[11] Ephesians 1:6–7 (NKJV): "[T]o the praise of the glory of His grace, by which He made us accepted in the Beloved. In Him we have redemption through His blood, the forgiveness of sins, according to the riches of his grace."

[12] Nouwen, *Lifesigns*, 36.

Chapter 9
Working through Relational Conflict

[1] Thomas Kelly, *Testament of Devotion* (San Francisco: Harper & Brothers, 1941), 61.

[2] Billy Graham, "10 Quotes from Billy Graham About His Wife," *The Billy Graham Library*, August 2, 2019, accessed May 14, 2025, https://billygrahamlibrary.org/blog-10-quotes-from-billy-graham-about-his-wife/.

[3] Quentin J. Schultze, *Communicating for Life: Christian Stewardship in Community and Media, Upd. & Exp.* (Pasco, WA: Integratio Press, 2024), 34.

[4] Jonathan Pettigrew and Diane Badzinski, *Family Communication and the Christian Faith: An Introduction and Exploration* (Pasco, WA: Integratio, 2023), 104.

[5] Frank E. X. Dance and Carl E. Larson, *Speech Communication: Concepts and Behaviors* (New York: Holt, Reinhart, and Winston, 1972), 56.

[6] Friends tend not to discuss their friendship. C. S. Lewis makes this point in *The Four Loves* where he maintains that it's *eros*—the romantic type of love—that is most consumed in understanding the state of the relationship. See C.S. Lewis, *The Four Loves* (San Diego: Hartcourt Brace & Company, 1988).

[7] Brian J. Willoughby, "Marriage is Increasingly an Institution of the Highly Religious: Why That Might Be a Problem," *Institute for Family Studies (IFS)*, September 13, 2022, https://ifstudies.org/blog/marriage-is-increasingly-an-institution-of-the-highly-religious-why-that-might-be-a-problem#:~:text=Almost%20universal%20data%20now%20show,of%20marriages%20documented%20each%20year.

[8] Taffy Brodesser-Akner, "The Year of Taylor Swift," *The Daily*, December 15, 2023, https://www.nytimes.com/2023/12/15/podcasts/the-daily/the-year-of-taylor-swift.html?showTranscript=1.

[9] "51 Best Sad Love Songs for a Broken Heart," *Glamour*, February 11, 2020, https://www.glamour.com/story/best-sad-love-songs-for-a-broken-heart.

[10] Swift appeared on the cover of TIME magazine three times, then as TIME'S Person of the Year in 2024. Her album, *The Tortured Poets Department* is her most recent project.

[11] "Glamour, "51 Best Sad Love Songs."

[12] Donny Hathaway and Roberta Flack (1971), "Where is the love?" [January 22,

2023] https://www.youtube.com/watch?v=ZcHPNUN-U8Ehttps://www.glamour.com/story/best-sad-love-songs-for-a-broken-heart.

[13] Paul A. Soukup, *Out of Eden* (Boston: Pauline Books, 2007).

[14] Soukup, *Out of Eden*, 38.

[15] Thomas Merton, *Love and Living* (San Francisco: Harper One, 2002), 38.

[16] Ephesians 4:26 (NIV): "'In your anger do not sin': Do not let the sun go down while you are still angry."

[17] 1 Peter 5:6 (NRSV): "Humble yourselves, therefore, under the mighty hand of God and He will exalt you in due time."

Chapter 10
Addressing Chaos in Relationships

[1] Online Etymology Dictionary, "Humility (n.)," from the Latin, *hummilitas*. Literally: "from the earth." [August 10, 2024] https://www.etymonline.com/word/humility.

[2] Galatians 5:25 (KJV). Paul reminds the young believers in Galatia, "If we live in the Spirit, let us also walk in the Spirit."

[3] Paul Rayburn, Host (Conversation with Antonio Damasio), "How Does the Brain Decide Who to Trust," July 24, 2009, *Science Friday*, produced by National Public Radio (NPR), *Talk of the Nation*. 7:46, https://www.npr.org/2009/07/24/106974470/how-does-the-brain-decide-who-to-trust.

[4] *Alcoholics Anonymous Big Book*, 4th ed. (New York: Alcoholics Anonymous World Services, 2002).

[5] Robert McGee, *Search for Significance: Seeing Your True Worth Through God's Eyes* (Nashville: Thomas Nelson, 2003), 98.

[6] Gus Cooney, Erica Boothy, and Mariana Lee, "The Thought Gap After Conversation: Underestimating the Frequency of Others' Thoughts About Us," *Journal of Experimental Psychology: General* 151, no. 5 (2022): 1069–1088, https://doi.org/10.1037/xge0001134.

[7] The inner voice is synonymous with the notion of "self-talk," and is sometimes referred to as "inner dialogue." It involves the stories we tell ourselves about what's going on in the external world, as well as an ongoing (but often unaware) commentary. For a closer look at intrapersonal communication, see L. Barker and Gordon Wiseman, "A Model of Intrapersonal Communication," *Journal of Communication* 16, no. 3 (September 1966): 172–179, https://doi.org/10.1111/j.1460-2466.1966.tb00031.x.

[8] Ecclesiastes 4:12b (NLT). The triple braided cord of Ecclesiastes is strong, bound together through the plaiting of a woman's hair. Such is the strength of a relationship that has the love of Christ interwoven through their priorities, language, and action.

[9] Martin Buber believed that human flourishing is directly connected to our ability to relate to others. His major work is the classic *I and Thou* (Princeton, NJ: Princeton University Press, 1949).

[10] Corey Anton, Student Publication, *Wide-Eyed* 1, no. 3 (June 2008): 21.

[11] Colossians 3:12 (NIV): "Therefore, as God's chosen people, holy and dearly loved, clothe yourselves with compassion, kindness, humility, gentleness, and patience." For further study, see Galatians 3:27 where Paul reminds Christ-followers that a life of faith means more than merely believing in Christ. It means we take on a new identity and seek to walk in the same ways as Jesus, full of compassion, humility, kindness, and love.

Chapter 11
Finding Strength and Solace in Solitude

[1] Dietrich Bonhoeffer, *Life Together: A Discussion of Christian Fellowship* (New York: Harper Row Publishers, 1954), 90–109. *Life Together* was written to the underground church in Germany. It was intended as a manual to help young seminarians understand that true leadership comes from serving, preferring, and loving each other in a life that's shared instead of isolated. Bonhoeffer focused on the centrality of Christ and the Church as a community of love.

[2] Ecclesiastes 3:7 (NIV). The full verse reads: "To everything there is a season, [. . .] a time to tear and a time to mend, a time to be silent and a time to speak."

[3] James 3:1–6 makes this tendency toward self-justification clear. We may not say we're perfect nor even consciously believe that we're perfect, but never backing down in a disagreement is more than a personality tic. It points to the perception we have of ourselves as perfect.

[4] Bonhoeffer, *Life Together*, 78.

[5] Bonhoeffer directed his teaching about religion-less Christianity to the young seminarians he mentored in the underground seminary of Finkenwalde.

[6] Judee K. Burgoon, David B. Buller, Jerold L. Hale, and Mark A. de Turck, "Relational Messages Associated with Nonverbal Behaviors," *Human Communication Research* 10, no. 3 (March 1984): 351–78.

[7] Dallas Willard, *The Spirit of the Disciplines: Understanding How God Changes Lives* (New York: Harper One, 1999), 210.

[8] Max Picard, *World of Silence* (Chicago: Regnery, 1989), 56.

[9] Eric Brende, *Better Off: Flipping the Switch on Technology* (New York: Harper-Collins, 2004), 158.

[10] Picard, *World of Silence*, 21.

[11] Thomas Merton, *Love and Living* (San Francisco: Harper One, 2002), 20.

[12] This is a reference to John 16:13–14 (NASB). The context here has to do with the apostle's query regarding Jesus's news of his need to leave them. John quotes Jesus as saying, "But when He, the Spirit of Truth comes, He will guide you into all truth; for He won't speak on his own initiative, but whatever He hears He will speak. And He will disclose to you what is to come" (vv. 13–14). Along with the comfort these words bring to Christ-followers, they provide an inkling to the importance of listening for the Voice of the Holy Spirit in our everyday life. The Spirit of God did not just inspire the words of Scripture but continues to inspire as He speaks to and through His people.

[13] Thomas Merton, "Love and Need: Is Love a Package or a Message?" in *The Reach of Dialogue*, ed. Rob Anderson, Kenneth N. Cissna, and Ronald C. Arnett (Cresskill, NJ: Hampton Press, 1994), x–xi.

Chapter 12
Powering Relationships with Prayer

[1] Philippians 4:6 (NIV): "Do not be anxious about anything, but in every situation, by prayer and petition, with thanksgiving, present your requests to God."

[2] Galatians 5:22–23 (NIV): "But the fruit of the Spirit is love, joy, peace, forbearance, kindness, goodness, faithfulness, gentleness, and self-control. Against such things there is no law."

[3] Isaiah 40:31 (NKJV): "But those who wait on the Lord shall renew their strength:

they shall mount up with wings like eagles, they shall run and not be weary, they shall walk and not faint."

[4] Paul A. Soukup, *Out of Eden* (Boston: Pauline Books, 2007), 39.

[5] John 5:19 (NKJV). This verse records Jesus saying, "Most assuredly, I say to you, the Son can do nothing of Himself, but what He sees the Father do; for whatever He does, the Son also does in like manner." Other passages that refer to this include John 5:30, John 8:28, and John 12:49–50.

[6] Jacques Ellul, *Prayer and Modern Man*, trans. C. Edward Hopkin (New York: Seabury, 1979), 144.

[7] Ellul, *Prayer and Modern Man*, 134.

[8] Henri Nouwen, *Bringing Prayer into Your Life with Open Hands* (New York: Ballentine Books, 1972), 54.

[9] Ellul, *Prayer and Modern Man*, 117.

[10] Understanding the place of prayer in communicating love brings us once again to the importance of silence as a communicational tool, for it is in the solitude of quiet presence with God that our hearts are often most open. It is there, in solitude, that we may best be able to perceive our own need for compassion, thus creating greater space and ability to listen with compassionate ears and a heart that makes room for human weakness. For excellent reading on this subject see the large corpus of books by Henri Nouwen.

[11] Thomas R. Kelly, *A Testament of Devotion* (New York: Harper & Brothers, 1941), 97.

[12] Vivek Murthy, *Our Epidemic of Loneliness and Isolation* (U.S. Department of Health and Human Services, Washington, DC. 2023), https://www.hhs.gov/sites/default/files/surgeon-general-social-connection-advisory.pdf.

[13] John 8:12 (NIV): "When Jesus spoke again to the people, he said, 'I am the light of the world. Whoever follows me will never walk in darkness but will have the light of life.'"

Index